12-DAY
Nativity

Hpe this helps your family celebrate the savior this year!

Marilee Woodfield

12-DAY
Nativity

Marilee Woodfield

Christmas Activities
— for a —
Christ-Centered Home

Plain Sight Publishing • An Imprint of Cedar Fort, Inc. • Springville, Utah

ISBN 13: 978-1-4621-1736-9

Published by Plain Sight Publishing, an imprint of Cedar Fort, Inc.,
2373 W. 700 S., Springville, UT 84663
Distributed by Cedar Fort, Inc., www.cedarfort.com

LIBRARY OF CONGRESS CATALOGING-IN-PUBLICATION DATA

Woodfield, Marilee Whiting, author.
12-day Nativity : Christmas activities for a Christ-centered home / Marilee Woodfield.
pages cm
Activities and crafts that celebrate Christmas with the traditional figures from holiday nativity sets.
Includes bibliographical references.
ISBN 978-1-4621-1736-9 (perfect bound : alk. paper)
1. Christmas decorations. 2. Jesus Christ--Nativity. 3. Crèches (Nativity scenes) 4. Handicraft. I. Title. II. Title: Twelve-day Nativity : Christmas activities for a Christ-centered home.
TT900.C4W66 2015
745.594'12--dc23
                    2015020713

Edited by Eileen Leavitt
Cover and page design by Lauren Error
Cover design © 2015 by Lyle Mortimer

Printed in the United States of America

10 9 8 7 6 5 4 3 2 1

Printed on acid-free paper

To Craig, who supports my
nativity obsession in every way

Contents

Introduction • VIII

Day 1: Are We Ready for the Baby? • 1

Day 2: Stable • 5

Day 3: Mary • 9

Day 4: Joseph • 15

Day 5: Donkey • 23

Day 6: Shepherd • 27

Day 7: Sheep • 33

Day 8: Angel • 37

Day 9: Star • 43

Day 10: Camel • 49

Day 11: Wise Men • 53

Day 12: Baby Jesus • 59

Nativity Pageant • 62

Nativity Dress-Up • 64

Putting It All Together • 72

Neighborhood Celebrations • 75

Advents • 77

Other Ways to Celebrate the Nativity • 92

Celebrating the Nativity around the World • 99

Nativity Books • 105

Notes • 109

Journal • 111

About the Author • 131

Introduction

Ever since St. Francis of Assisi first began the tradition, families and communities have celebrated the Christmas season by displaying nativities to illustrate the Christmas story. While Santa's popularity has grown, so has the commercialized Christmas, and by extension, so has the feeling of anxiety many of us have while we focus less on experiencing Christmas and more on purchasing it.

- Last year as you celebrated Christmas, what was your greatest moment of joy? Was it when you remembered the birth of the Savior, or was it when you succeeded at securing that one hard-to-find gift?

- Are you exhausted from the long laundry list of things to do to create the perfect tablescape, the perfect party, or the perfect cookie tray for the neighborhood get-together, or are you exhausted from serving others as the Savior did?

- Are you so busy preparing Christmas for your family that you don't have time to celebrate it with them?

In this book, you'll find activities that you can use to prepare to celebrate the Nativity story and fill your home with the spirit of Christmas as a result. This book includes the following:

- suggestions for celebrating each character in the Nativity story one day at a time

- a template to create your own Nativity scene or Advent calendar

- directions for creating or performing your own simple Nativity using family and friends to depict the key characters and events of the Nativity

- information and related activities on how other countries celebrate the Nativity

- recommendations for other Nativity-related events that will help bring the true meaning of Christmas into your home

Whether you choose to do one activity a day in the twelve days leading up to or after Christmas (for traditionalists) or just choose to do a select few, you can use this book as a guide to help you decide how much celebrating makes sense for your family. The ultimate goal is for you to have a spirit-filled, family-friendly holiday season with Jesus Christ as the central part of your Christmas.

The Story of the Nativity

In Luke 1:1–4, Luke prefaces the intent of his writing. These verses suggest that his writings are a "declaration of those things which are most surely believed among us." He expresses his own "perfect understanding" and hopes that we "mightest know the certainty of those things." The Nativity narrative most commonly taught today has been constructed by combining Luke and Matthew's accounts. (Luke focuses on Mary and the virgin birth, while Matthew focuses on Jesus's lineage, Joseph, and the visit from the Wise Men.) In the traditional narrative, we have added our own insertions and assumptions (donkeys, camels, and so on) to fill in the story, though none are mentioned in the scriptural text.

There are no known firsthand accounts of the birth of the Savior. The Gospels were recorded many years after Christ's ministry and death. We do know from the account of Luke that the shepherds went and told all about the miraculous event, but Mary kept all these things in her heart (Luke 2:19). So it is likely that the events described in the two Gospels are accounts that have been passed from person to person before they were recorded (see Luke 1:2).

Many biblical scholars look at the Gospels not as historical accounts intended to create facts and timelines of events but rather as religious texts whose value is in testifying of the Savior and His divinity. We are often confused and frustrated when we try to apply our twenty-first century sensibilities (science and facts) to ancient lives and cultures and then try to assign context and motivations based on our current cultural norms.

Even the date that we celebrate the birth of the baby Jesus (December 25) was a construct of the church, chosen centuries after Jesus had lived.

So whether you believe in the story literally as told in the Gospels of Luke and Matthew or you believe the story to be symbolic, the absence of evidence leaves us with our faith. Because there isn't DNA evidence or a paper trail to support the details, it forces us to weigh our hearts and choose to believe. Perhaps this is all in the design of God, knowing and wanting us to exercise faith in His birth, His life, and His divinity. And isn't the Nativity story all about faith and hope?

Note from the Author

The Nativity is not just a story about Joseph, Mary, and baby Jesus. It is not just a story about nameless shepherds, angels, or Wise Men. Neither is it just a story of overcrowded inns, starry nights, or long journeys. It is a story of God keeping His promise. It is a story of God using ordinary people to do extraordinary things. And most of all, it is a story of God's love for you and me. While the birth of the Savior was not an ordinary birth, what made it remarkable was the way the Savior lived His life. It is remarkable, and we remember and celebrate it centuries later across many countries and cultures because Jesus suffered in Gethsemane, died on the cross, and rose again.

The purpose of this book is to give you ideas—lots of them—to help share that story with your family, friends, neighbors, and others you may meet upon your path. Even with wholesome family activities, it's still easy to become overwhelmed by the season. So while you consider how to celebrate the 12-Day Nativity, please remember that there's no one right way of participating. Don't feel pressure to recreate someone else's traditions or do something just because it is suggested. Do what works for your family. Celebrate just a few days or combine or skip days as your schedule permits. Consider this as permission to abandon anything materialistic or time-consuming that drags you down (whether that be a current tradition you celebrate or a suggestion in this book). The important thing is that you are working at turning your heart toward Jesus, and if you're doing that, you're doing it right.

Make It Your Own

The scriptures used in this book were taken from the King James Version of the Bible. You may have other scriptures or stories from your own faith tradition that add to the 12-Day Nativity experience. Feel free to substitute scriptures, songs, and devotional thoughts to make your 12-Day Nativity unique to your family. You may need to adapt the activities to meet the needs of younger or older children to make it fun for everyone.

Remember that the whole purpose of celebrating the story of the Nativity is remembering that, in the end, it really isn't just a story; it is so much more.

Nativity Origins

As a child, I remember having one family nativity set that was displayed each year. It was a simple white set made of plaster, and the stable was built out of scrap wood and leftover paneling from our 1970s-chic basement. The set always sat perched on top of the piano, surrounded by twinkle lights covered with angel hair (a spun-glass product that is hairlike and white-translucent). The figures were not heavy, and it was always a challenge to find a spot where they would stand up in between the lights and angel hair. Over the years, our family nativity grew in "character" as heads were broken off and reglued. The shepherds and Wise Men were referred to as the "German shepherds" and "wise guys." My sister affectionately labeled the sheep as "cheats" before she could pronounce them otherwise. I was more concerned about the naked baby Jesus and exasperated my mother as every time she passed the nativity, she would find a dirty old rag or handkerchief covering Him. When she finally discovered the responsible party, I explained that I thought the baby Jesus must be cold, and so I made it my mission to cover Him up.

Somehow, the family's nativity set ended up at the home of one of my brothers and was saved from the Goodwill pile by my sister-in-law, who knew I had been collecting nativities. It had come to them as a white-elephant gift exchange between siblings a few years prior, and it had been abandoned on a basement storage shelf for a few years. The stable is now warped, and I have to reset the nails every year. The figures have been broken and reglued many times, leaving one to wonder what horrific tale of carnage they would tell. It is by no means the most beautiful nativity in our home, but it is one of my favorites. First, as a symbol of happy Christmases past. Second, it reminds me of my relationship with the Savior: broken and fixed many times over—warped, not pretty, but loved and beloved just the same.

I began collecting nativities several years ago when I became involved in an interfaith community nativity exhibit that was hosted at my church. In a matter of a few days, the church is transformed from bare walls and empty spaces to an amazing display of hundreds of nativities from around the world. It is an exhausting experience, as a small army of volunteers drapes tables and boxes in yards of fabric and miles of garland and twinkle lights. Then, each nativity is carefully unwrapped and placed for display. Each nativity set (or *crèche*, as they are often called) is a symbolic representation of both the artist's and the owner's testimony of the birth of the Savior.

If you don't already have a family nativity set, perhaps this is the year to search for the perfect display for your home. My sister has one nativity set for each family member, and they alone (no presents) are displayed under the Christmas tree until Christmas day—a reminder that the birth of the Savior is the greatest gift of the season.

Check your local listings for nativity displays in your area, and take an afternoon or evening to go and view them together as a family.

12-Day Nativity

Throughout much of the world, the Twelve days of Christmas are actually celebrated starting on Christmas day and ending twelve days later on the day of Epiphany. When I was growing up, however, our family had a tradition of celebrating the twelve days of leading up to Christmas Day. Our Twelve Days of Christmas involved choosing a neighbor or someone in our church community who we felt needed a little extra Christmas cheer. Then, beginning on December 13, we would deliver a small gift or goodie anonymously each day until Christmas Eve. I don't remember much of the details of those days, but I do remember learning all the tricks of the drop-and-run: where to hide, how not to leave fresh tracks in the snow to be easily traced, and which doors we really had to sprint to in order to not get caught, and those we could casually saunter away from without threat of discovery.

There were many good feelings and poignant memories that came out of that experience, particularly the year that we did the Twelve Days of Christmas for the church janitor. He was a recent widower, and he quickly learned our pattern of dropping and running, so it became a challenge for us kids to deliver the goods and get out of sight before he could get to the door. He opened the door so quickly on some nights that I am certain he was waiting for us. I don't know if he ever found out whom it was that was leaving him a nightly gift of love (I suspect he did, but my parents did a good job of letting us believe otherwise). But the tale is often retold of the last night, Christmas Eve, where he stood a little longer in the cold night, his tall but aged frame silhouetted through the open door by the lights within and called out into the winter air, "Thank you, whoever you are!"

I had such fond memories of this tradition as a child that my husband and I celebrated the Twelve Days of Christmas with our children when we started our family. I have to admit that it was a far different experience from a parent's perspective because it required a lot of work to prepare each day's package and note of explanation—usually written in a witty poem. Then we rallied the occasionally reluctant kids into the car while they argued over who had to get out and make the drop. As our family grew and our schedules became increasingly complicated, there were years when I remembered a day late and we found ourselves dropping off two days at a time, or I would leave a package in the morning after dropping the kids at school or on my way to work. Some nights, we delivered so late, we simply left the box or bag on the doorstep in the hopes that it would still be there in the morning. Far from my cherubic memories as a child, I hoped that all the effort would make some difference for someone. I'm sure that part of the problem was that I was trying to create something for my kids that they weren't invested in. I fell into the habit of doing it all myself (often resenting it) and wondering why my kids hadn't caught the spirit of the tradition. If I had to do it over again, I would do some things differently so that my children could own more of the process instead of just being the delivery kids. I was trying to teach them to serve without actually require them to do much serving other than to get out of the car.

I think the year my children will remember the most is the year that we did the Twelve Days of Christmas for four elderly ladies who all lived in the same apartment complex. We did not count on them sharing their experience with one another, and we soon learned that when we delivered to the first home, she would call and warn the others that we were coming. It became quite a challenge for my then-twelve-year-old son to figure out how to outwit the four of them and remain anonymous. We still tease him that, as big and smart as he is, he isn't fast enough to outrun a bunch of old ladies who caught him in the act one night.

The 12-Day Nativity is engineered similarly, but instead of random goodies and gifts, one figure of the nativity is brought out each day until the *crèche* is complete, with baby Jesus as the last to arrive. As you celebrate with your family, you may also want to share the 12-Day Nativity with a friend or neighbor who you think might also enjoy a little holiday spirit sometime throughout the season.

You may choose to mix and match activities as they fit your schedule, personal preferences, and tolerance for holiday insanity. You may also wish to add figures to your *crèche* in a different order than suggested. The key to making this a successful experience is to make your home a little more Christ-centered, so feel free to tailor it to your family's needs. Included in each day's plan is the following:

-  a scripture passage or two from the Bible about that character and his or her place in the Nativity story, as told in the Gospels

- 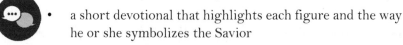 a song you can sing or listen to together (words are provided, and musical accompaniment can be found online)

- 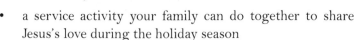 a short devotional that highlights each figure and the way he or she symbolizes the Savior

- a service activity your family can do together to share Jesus's love during the holiday season

- 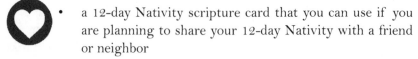 a 12-day Nativity scripture card that you can use if you are planning to share your 12-day Nativity with a friend or neighbor

- a Christlike attribute to focus on and develop throughout the Christmas season and throughout the year as your gift to the Savior

- activities associated with each Nativity character (many are intended for simple family fun and togetherness and are not specifically spiritually inclined)

You will need a nativity set with the following pieces: a stable, Mary, Joseph, baby Jesus, a sheep, a shepherd, an angel, a star, Wise Men, a donkey, and a camel.

Keep It Simple

The idea behind the 12-Day Nativity is that you present one character each day and add it to your nativity scene. There are lots of suggestions and ways in which you can accomplish this, but to keep this from also being another one of those harried and stressful activities, keep it simple, and consider which activities you want to do together as a family. As you celebrate each day, and as your nativity *crèche* fills up, remember that the purpose is to be together each day as a family. I hope that you won't just add this on top of what you are already doing but that it will inspire you to let go of those traditions or activities that are pulling you apart and help you to refocus your family and fill your home with Jesus's love. Alternate between fun games and service activities. If it feels like you've just added one more thing to your list of things to do during the busy holiday season, you may want to consider giving up something less Christ-centered. Are there traditions that you are spending a lot of time, energy, and money on that really have no value for your family other than "we always do this"?

Here are some other ideas for simplifying your 12-Day Nativity:

Remember. Keep a notebook or list of things that worked well or didn't seem to fit for you. This way, you'll know what to avoid next year. Often, my best ideas come after the fact. So if you're like me, and inspiration hits after you have celebrated the 12-Day Nativity, write it down and keep it for next year. I promise you won't remember if you don't write it down! We've included a journal section at the back of this book just in case. Use it to record any successes or failures.

Keep a 12-Day Nativity Box. Collect a large box, and keep all the supplies and activities that you use this year in one place so that when you're ready to celebrate again next year, you're good to go!

Prepare ahead. If you're one of those people who has all your Christmas shopping done by October and the tree up and decorated by Thanksgiving, this is not news for you. For those of us who always seem to be flying by the seat of our pants (you know who you are—the mom who parks in the fire lane and dashes into the school just in time to see the third-grade musical), make a plan to get everything else done before you begin celebrating the 12-Day Nativity. If you must take beautifully decorated cookies to the neighbors, do it on the first of December, not the twenty-fourth! Make a list of all the must-do's, and set a deadline to do them *before* you begin the 12-Day Nativity so you can just enjoy the holiday. Yes, the stress of getting everything done will still be there, but think how much more enjoyable Christmas will be if you actually get to sit back and celebrate it! If that's just not possible, consider celebrating the 12-Day Nativity during the actual Twelve Days of Christmas that start on Christmas Day. It'll be a great way to extend the Christmas spirit into the New Year—if you're not completely burnt out by then!

Sharing the 12-Day Nativity

You may wish to share your love for the Savior with a friend or neighbor this Christmas season. Instead of a plate of cookies and a note proclaiming your devotion, why not share an additional nativity and a *12-Day Nativity* book with him or her? You can also share the 12-Day Nativity by inviting other families to celebrate with you by having them come to your home as you engage in one of the suggested activities.

You can do the 12-Day Nativity as a doorbell-ditching experience, leaving another family to wonder who is leaving the love, or you may want to reveal yourself and start a conversation with your friends about how they celebrate the Nativity in their home or faith tradition. If you do choose to share the 12-Day Nativity with your friend or neighbor, you might want to start with this book, a small decorated box with the "Greatest Gift" gift tag (see page XIX for a version you can copy), and a printed version of the Nativity story. (Luke 1:26–39, Luke 2: 1–20, Matthew 1:18–25, and Matthew 2:1–12 give the most complete text. You may wish to simplify it.) You may also want to leave a little note in the box, letting them know to watch their porch in the coming days for more gifts of the Savior. As you capture the spirit of the 12-Day Nativity, you'll likely want to share this way of celebrating the true meaning of Christmas with many friends and associates. Just be cautious to not let your zeal for sharing God's word with others make you so busy that it keeps you from enjoying it in your own home! Keep it simple, and allow for flexibility and for God to speak to your heart.

There are lots more ideas about celebrating with family, friends, and neighbors on page 75.

Before You Celebrate Your 12-Day Nativity

To prepare for celebrating the 12-Day Nativity, begin by reading the entire story (found in Luke 2 and Matthew) or by telling it in your own words on a level that your family will understand.

To introduce the story, place a Bible in a small box, along with any illustrations you may want to use. You can use one of the books listed in the "Nativity Book" reading section (see page 105) or use the illustrations of the nativity characters (see pages 95–97) to help retell the story. Wrap the box in simple paper (this isn't the time for Santa or the Grinch) and tie it up with a bow. Use the "Greatest Gift" gift tag (see page XIX), and attach it to the package. Find a time to sit down as a family at the beginning of the holiday season. You might want to create a cozy atmosphere—something different and special, such as telling the story by candlelight or near a lit Christmas tree (turn the rest of the lights in the room off). Show the box and tell them that there is a special gift inside. Have each family member share about one of the best gifts they have ever received. Next, have them think about and tell about a time when they gave a gift and how that made them feel. Have the family members guess what might be in the box. You can give hints if needed, such as, "This is the greatest gift ever. It's not a toy and can't be bought with money."

Read the gift tag and talk about what the scripture from John 3:16 means—how God loved each of us so much that He gave the best gift He could: the Savior. Then share the story from the Bible. Don't worry if they've heard it before; repetition will help them to remember and will also help them to see discrepancies from the Bible text and retellings that we see, read, or watch that may take creative license with the story. Remind your family that the reason why Jesus's birth was so important was because it was the first step in the plan for our Heavenly Father to provide us a Savior. The reason why we still tell the story of the Savior's birth is because of the way He lived His life and because of His gift of love, grace, and redemption. Leave the box and the pictures opened under the tree so your children can revisit and retell the story over and over as you celebrate the 12-Day Nativity.

As you introduce each figure of the nativity, consider doing it in a similar way and time each night, right before or after dinner, right before bedtime, first thing in the morning, and so on. Just find a time that is quiet, where you won't have to spend all your energy regathering the family from various activities and from all four corners of the house. If you are going to wrap each figure, consider doing it in the same box or in similar packaging so that by the second or third day, the kids will know what to expect when they see the box. Place the package out in the morning and leave it there all day to build anticipation. Have them guess which figure might be in the box before opening it each day.

Share a thought, and add the character to your nativity scene. Light a candle each day as you retell the parts of the story to introduce the characters. You can light the previous candles and then add that day's candle. At the end of the twelve days, you'll have twelve candles burning brightly.

Keep a Journal

A great way to savor the treasured memories that you will have while celebrating the 12-Day Nativity is to take lots of pictures (or hand your phone or camera over to your kids to get their point of view). You can combine them into a scrapbook or keepsake memento each year. Next year as you begin your 12-Day Nativity, you'll have your own stories and pictures to reflect upon as you celebrate each day. Be sure to include anecdotes and summaries of each day's activities as well as the fun things you'll overhear your kids say or share as they talk about their experiences while celebrating the 12-Day Nativity. If you continue this tradition year after year, this memory journal itself will become a treasured part of your holiday celebration.

12-Day Nativity Scripture Cards

Use these nativity cards as a gift tag if you are presenting the 12-Day Nativity as a gift. Just attach the card to the package or wrapping for each day that you deliver. Here are some other uses for the scripture cards:

Angel

Luke 2:10
And the angel said unto them, Fear not: for, behold, I bring you good tidings of great joy.

- Print out the scripture cards and cut, stack, and bind the pages together to create a coloring book.

- Enlarge each card, and color and frame them to create a tabletop reminder of each day's nativity character.

- Make several copies of the cards to use for simple games like memory matching games or Go Fish.

- Use them to create Christmas greeting cards or gift thank-you cards.

Kitchen Table Devotional

Use the nativity character scripture cards (see pages XX–XLIII) around the house. Enlarge each individual picture and color it (or have one of the kids do it). Place the enlarged scripture card in a picture frame and display it in a prominent area of your home, such as the kitchen countertop or on the door to the garage or next to the TV—wherever it will be seen often as a reminder of the day's character and the daily devotional.

Gifts for Him

As you talk about the Nativity each day, focus on one gift or characteristic that you want to share with the Savior. Character traits that emulate those of the Savior are suggested for each day, although you may, of course, wish to think of your own. Along with the scripture card, print "Gift for Him" notes (page 61) for each person. Write down your gift and something you will do that day to become more like the Savior. For example, when celebrating the donkey, whose Christlike characteristic is "helpful," think of one way that you can be helpful to someone, or look for ways that others have been helpful to you. Write down what you plan to do, and then use the back of the card to write about what you did. Save these cards in a special stocking hung for the baby Jesus.

The Greatest Gift...

John 3:16

For God so loved the world, that he gave his only begotten Son, that whosoever believeth in him should not perish, but have everlasting life.

Bethlehem

Still

Find one way today to be quiet and still enough to feel God's love. Let go of one thing that causes you to be anxious, angry, or afraid.

Bethlehem

Bethlehem

Luke 2:4
And Joseph also went up from
Galilee, out of the city of Nazareth,
into Judea, unto the city of David,
which is called Bethlehem.

The Stable

Service

Find one way today to serve
someone in your family.

The Stable

Psalm 61:3
For thou hast been a shelter for me,
and a strong tower from the enemy.

Mary

Ponder

Mary pondered and was thoughtful. Take a minute to ponder and pray. Write down what God speaks to your heart.

Mary

Mary

Luke 1:38
And Mary said, Behold the
handmaid of the Lord; be it unto
me according to thy word.

Donkey

Helpful

The donkey was helpful when
Mary was tired and needed to rest.
Find one way to be helpful or give
rest to someone else today.

Donkey

Donkey

Galatians 6:2
Bear ye one another's burdens,
and so fulfil the law of Christ.

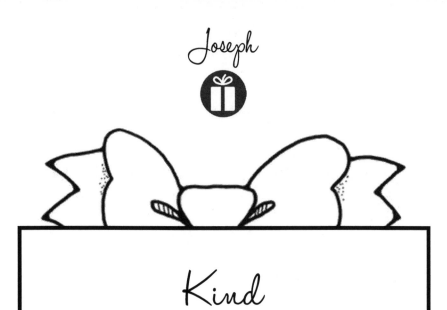

Kind

Joseph was kind. Find someone who needs some kindness or a friendly gesture today.

Joseph

Joseph

Matthew 1:24
Then Joseph being raised from
sleep did as the angel of the
Lord had bidden him.

Sheep

Willing

Sheep are known for their willingness to follow their master. Find one way today to act without having to be told to do something good or helpful.

Sheep

Sheep

John 10:27
My sheep hear my voice, and I
know them, and they follow me.

Shepherd

Humble

The shepherds were humble and
were willing to do what they
thought was right. Find one
time today where you can practice
being humble and teachable.

Shepherd

Shepherd

Luke 2:8
And there were in the same country
shepherds abiding in the field, keeping
watch over their flock by night.

Angel

Joyful

The angels and the heavenly hosts sang with joy at the good news. Find one thing to be joyful about today.

Angel

Luke 2:10
And the angel said unto them,
Fear not: for, behold, I bring you
good tidings of great joy.

Bethlehem Star

Guide

The star was the guide for the Wise Men to find the baby Jesus. Find one way to be an example of Jesus that will show others the way to be like Him.

Bethlehem Star

Matthew 2:9
And, lo, the star, which they
saw in the east, went before
them, till it came and stood over
where the young child was.

Wise Men

Seek

The Wise Men had been seeking or looking for the sign of the new King long before they began their journey. Find one way to seek out something about Jesus today.

Wise Men

Wise Men

Matthew 2:1
Behold, there came wise men
from the east to Jerusalem.

Camel

Endure

The camels carried heavy packs on their backs for the long journey. They had to simply endure the trail day by day. Find one thing today that you can be patient and endure, having faith that there is goodness and wonder at the end of the trail.

Camel

Camel

Matthew 24:13
He that shall endure unto the end,
the same shall be saved.

Pause

Take a minute today to pause and think about the Savior. Think of one way you are thankful for Him.

Baby Jesus

Luke 2:11
For unto you is born this day in
the city of David a Saviour,
which is Christ the Lord.

Day 1: Are We Ready for the Baby?

 Luke 2:1-7

 "O Little Town of Bethlehem" (melody can be found online)

O little town of Bethlehem,

How still we see thee lie.

Above thy deep and dreamless sleep,

The silent stars go by;

Yet in thy dark streets shineth

The everlasting Light,

The hopes and fears of all the years,

Are met in thee tonight.

O morning stars, together

Proclaim thy holy birth

And praises sing to God, the King,

And peace to men on earth.

As Mary and Joseph entered Bethlehem to be counted and taxed, it must have been quite a scene. Families from all over the region had descended upon the city for the same purpose, and as the story goes, there was no room for them at the inn. Luke 2 from the Bible begins the story this way:

1: And it came to pass in those days, that there went out a decree from Caesar Augustus, that all the world should be taxed.

2: (And this taxing was first made when Cyrenius was governor of Syria.)

3: And all went to be taxed, every one into his own city.

4: And Joseph also went up from Galilee, out of the city of Nazareth, into Judea, unto the city of David, which is called Bethlehem; (because he was of the house and lineage of David:)

5: To be taxed with Mary his espoused wife, being great with child.

6: And so it was, that, while they were there, the days were accomplished that she should be delivered.

7: And she brought forth her firstborn son, and wrapped him in swaddling clothes, and laid him in a manger; because there was no room for them in the inn.

This is the only place in the scriptural text that makes mention of an inn, and the words are small and simple: "there was no room for them in the inn." We don't know how many doors Joseph might have knocked on that night, trying to seek shelter for Mary, but they probably searched out more than one inn and knocked on more than one door before the little family was resigned to a stable.

While most nativity sets don't include the innkeeper, we're going to start our 12-Day Nativity at the inn in Bethlehem. If the people of Bethlehem had known who Mary carried, would they have been more accommodating for the new little family? Would the innkeepers have been more inclined to clear a space for the soon-to-be Savior of the World? As a family, are we ready in our hearts for Jesus? Jesus was a great example of being openhearted toward those who were in need. Just like the innkeepers in Bethlehem, we have a choice in whether we let the Savior into our lives and into our homes.

Set the Table

As a fun tradition, set a specific table setting in honor of the Savior. You can choose whether your place setting will be simple or grandiose, but include all the family in setting up one portion of the table setting. Talk about preparing our homes and hearts for the Savior to come and be with us. Leave this place setting at the table with an empty seat throughout the Christmas season to remind you that Jesus needs a place with us, and we need to invite Him in!

Ready for the King

As a family, talk about what it means to be prepared to celebrate the coming of Jesus. If Jesus were coming to our house tomorrow, what might we do to prepare for Him? Allow each family member to give a suggestion. Someone might suggest preparing your home by decorating or picking up the clutter. Someone else might want to prepare a special treat. Maybe this is the day to decorate your nativity or tree. Make a list of your ideas, and then choose as many as you feel appropriate to do as a family to prepare for the upcoming Nativity experiences.

🪏 Come to Bethlehem

Supplies needed: cardboard boxes, colored paper, scissors or utility knife, crayons, markers, colored pencils or paint, adhesive tape, paper cups

As a family, build your own City of David (or Bethlehem). Each person can create one or two pieces of the city. Cut out windows and doorways, color each building, and add details such as trees and townspeople as desired. Place the Bethlehem city on a table or mantle and string twinkle lights throughout the buildings so the windows glow. Make sure the inn is the last building in the city.

Draw (or print) a picture of Mary and Joseph or use the nativity figures (see page 95–97). Attach the picture to an inverted cup, and place the Mary and Joseph figures at the edge of the city. Have the family give suggestions of things you can do to help or serve one another or friends and extended family members. As a family member shares thoughts of love and service, have them move Mary and Joseph one step closer to the inn.

Look to your community for opportunities to serve. Donating food to local food banks, making cookies for your local fire station, or even picking up trash in your neighborhood are all simple ways you can serve your "little town."

Day 2: Stable

Add the stable to your nativity scene.

 Psalm 61:3 For thou hast been a shelter for me, and a strong tower from the enemy.

 "In a Little Stable" (melody can be found online)

In a little stable

Far across the sea

Was a little Baby

Just like you and me.

Not a bed or cradle,

Not a pillow deep,

But a lowly manger

Was His place to sleep.

Shepherds stood around Him,

Angels watched with care,

For this Babe was Jesus,

Lying, smiling there.

Oh, I love this Jesus,

Who was little then.

For He surely loves me,

Little though I am.

Do I Have Room for Jesus in My Life?

In humble contrast to what we assume was going on in the inn, the stable provided a quiet refuge for Mary and Joseph. Did the innkeeper have any sense of what was to come? Did others who were staying at the inn take note of the new star? Why did the Wise Men and shepherds have to travel so far to honor the birth of the Christ child when there were so many others nearby? How much of God's work is going on right under our noses unnoticed because we're too busy, preoccupied, or uninterested? Take some time today to step away, be still, and listen. Ask to feel of God's love, and ask yourself, *Do I have room for Jesus in my life?*

Stable Storytime

Supplies needed: blankets, sheets, furniture, pillows, clothespins or other clamps, lamp, extension cord, flashlight or battery-operated lantern, favorite Nativity storybook.

Make a stable out of blankets by arranging furniture or chairs in a circle (make sure that it is large enough for the entire family to fit inside). Drape blankets or sheets to make a roof and sides. Clamp in place with clothespins. Place pillows and blankets on the floor and a small lamp or lantern inside. (Make sure to put it where it won't tip over and where small hands won't accidentally get burned on the lit bulb.) Have the whole family climb inside your stable and read your favorite Nativity storybook (see "Nativity Books," page 105) by the glow of the lantern. If your children are readers, have them read the story to you. Alternatively, if the night isn't too cold and you live near a wooded area (or you can hunker down under the playset at a local park), consider taking warm blankets, hot chocolate, and hand warmers to a cozy spot and having your Nativity storytime under the stars.

Hide-and-Seek Doors

Choose one person to be "it." While the rest of the family covers their eyes and counts to one hundred, the person who is it runs and hides behind a closed door somewhere in the house. When the rest of the family reaches the count of one hundred, they then go search for the person who is hiding by knocking on doors one at a time around the house. If someone knocks on the door, and no one answers, they should move on to another door. If they knock on a door and the person who is hiding on the inside opens the door, the person doing the seeking then comes quickly inside, and they hide together until all the family has found the right door. (The person who is hiding should always open the door if someone knocks on it.) Play again with a new person hiding this time.

Build a Stable

Supplies needed: craft sticks, tape or glue, paper cups, cardboard or other recyclables, stopwatch or timer

Using the supplies listed above, have family members compete to see who can build the best stable within a given time limit. (Start with a one-to-two-minute time limit at first, and then try a much longer time limit if needed.) Award prizes for the tallest, sturdiest, most creative, best use of tape, and so on. For older kids, allow them to work in teams, or see what they can build without any adhesive tape or glue.

 Just as the stable offered warmth and shelter, we can show our love to the Savior by offering the same to others. Today's service challenge is to find someone who needs God's love or to be sheltered from the world around them. Giving a warm hug, a kind word or deed, or a listening ear are all simple ways we can give others "shelter." Is there someone at school who seems lonely and needs a friend?

Just as Joseph and Mary sought shelter in the stable, many people today seek the same kind of shelter, and many communities offer temporary shelter for them. Locate a shelter for the homeless (or any other kind of shelter) in your community and find out what the needs are and what you can do as a family to donate or provide services. Include family, friends, neighbors or your church community if you find a need that is greater than what your family can do alone.

Day 3: Mary

Add Mary to the nativity scene.

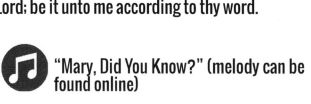 Luke 1:26-56

30: And the angel said unto her, Fear not, Mary: for thou hast found favour with God.

38: And Mary said, Behold the handmaid of the Lord; be it unto me according to thy word.

🎵 "Mary, Did You Know?" (melody can be found online)

Mary, did you know that your baby boy

would one day walk on water?

Mary, did you know that your baby boy

will save our sons and daughters?

Did you know that your baby boy

has come to make you new?

This child that you delivered

will soon deliver you.

Mary, did you know that your baby boy

will give sight to a blind man?

Mary, did you know that your baby boy

will calm the storm with His hand?

Mary did you know that your baby boy

has walked where angels trod?

When you kiss your little baby,

You've kissed the face of God?

Oh, Mary, did you know

The blind will see,

The deaf will hear,

The dead will live again,

The lame will leap,

The dumb will speak

The praises of the Lamb.

Mary, did you know that your baby boy

Is Lord of All Creation?

Mary, did you know that your baby boy

Would one day rule the nations?

Did you know that your baby boy

Is heaven's perfect Lamb?

The sleeping child you're holding

Is the Great I Am.

Can God Call on Me?

From the scriptural account, we know that Mary was highly favored of God (Luke 1:28). While there is no account of Mary leading up to the moment when the angel Gabriel appeared to her, we can imagine what kind of woman she must have been for God to choose her to be the mother of Jesus. Mary's response is interesting because she didn't protest the angel's words; she didn't claim to be unfit or unworthy. Her question was a matter of logistics and curiosity: "How shall this be, seeing I know not a man?" (Luke 1:34). The angel continued, telling Mary that "with God nothing shall be impossible" (Luke 1:37). Sometimes, we get so wrapped up in what we think can't happen that we forget what can happen when

we allow God room to direct our lives. She must have thought about how this could complicate her life and compromise her relationship with Joseph. There must have been many questions and concerns. But Mary humbly submitted to God's will. The Savior, too, is an example of submitting to His Father's will, even when the outcome seemed difficult or unsure.

How often do we ponder all the things God asks of us in our hearts (Luke 2:19) and then offer ourselves by simply saying, "Behold the handmaid of the Lord"? Are we offering God our whole hearts and souls willingly? Like Mary, are we on the right path so that when God needs us, He knows He can call on us?

Love from Mom

Supplies needed: markers or crayons, copies of "Mother, I love you" (page 13), index cards or slips of paper, large bowl

Mary is an example of a loving mother. Share stories with your family of your mother or someone else in your life who "mothered" you, encouraged you, or inspired you. Have each family member make a list of all the things that they have learned from their mother, what they love about their mother, or just a list of things they know their mother does for them that shows them that she loves them. Do a similar activity for a grandmother. Compile all the thoughts into a small scrapbook. Have the children draw pictures or add family photos of your mother or grandmother to complete the book. Use the "Mother, I love you" coloring page (see page 13) to write notes of love or draw pictures for your mother, grandmother, or other beloved mother figure.

Variation: Use this time to honor your mother. Make her favorite dinner and let her tell stories about her childhood, things she liked to do, what her favorite color was, her favorite book, her best birthday ever, memories of family vacations, and so on. Have the kids generate the questions and place each one on an index card or slip of paper. Fold it in half and place it in a bowl. Have Mom draw one card at a time and answer the questions. Be sure to record (video or write down) all the stories.

"Mother, May I . . ."

Choose one person to be "it." Start with Mom, if you prefer, and then allow other family members to take her place and act as "Mom." Have Mom sit on one end of the room and everyone else start on the other. Each person, in turn, requests permission from Mom to move forward a number of steps. The catch is that they must say, "Mother, may I move three [or any other number] steps please?" If they don't say *please*, then Mother flatly refuses their request. If she accepts their request, she then grants them permission but also makes a request of her own. In addition to moving forward the number of steps requested, Mom suggests a certain way in which she wants them to move. For example, she might ask them to please move using three crab steps, robot steps, gorilla steps, ballerina steps, and so on. Mom can also make the game more interesting by suggesting that they may move three steps, but it has to be backward or sideways, or the steps can be giant steps, baby steps, or normal steps. Continue taking turns requesting and enjoying the silly ways Mom is making the family move until everyone reaches Mom, and a new "Mom" is chosen and the game begins again.

Swaddle the Baby

Supplies needed: small toy babies or stuffed animals, long strips of fabric or toilet paper rolls

Baby Jesus was wrapped in swaddling clothes. Swaddling clothes are similar to a blanket or long strips of fabric that help keep the baby warm and tucked in tight so they feel safe and secure. Give each family member a doll or stuffed animal and a roll or length of fabric strips. (Make sure everyone has the same length of fabric.) At the "go" signal, everyone wraps up their doll as quickly as possible, using all the fabric strips. The first person to wrap the baby wins. You may want to add extra challenges for older players (the doll's face must be showing, the ends must be tucked in, and so on).

Variation: Divide the family into two or three groups. (Depending on the size of your family, this works best in small groups of two to three.) Have one person be the "baby," while the other team members use toilet paper to "swaddle" the baby. At the "go" signal, teams work together as fast as they can to completely wrap up the baby with the toilet paper. The first team to do so wins. Reorganize the teams and play again.

Variation: Wrap up one of the team members tightly in a blanket, and then challenge the rest of the team to move the swaddled team member from one room to another. This will take some creativity to move a swaddled dad, who will be significantly more difficult to move, than a smaller teammate. Make it into a relay where the first swaddled teammate is moved to one room then switches places with another teammate, who is swaddled and transported to a second room. Race to see which team can swaddle and transport their team the fastest.

 Research to find the many different women's shelters that serve your community. Find out what their needs are, and have your family work to meet one of those needed either by yourselves or by pooling the collective talents and skills of other families in your circle of friends, neighbors, coworkers, or church community. You might be able to provide clothing, bedding, other needed items, or just flowers or a fragrant wreath to bring a little love and cheer.

If there is no women's shelter or charity in your community, talk with your pastor or clergyman and ask if there is anything you can do for the Lord by serving more diligently as a family in the church.

"Mother, I Love You" Coloring Page

Day 4: Joseph

Add Joseph to the nativity scene.

 Matthew 1:20, 24-25

20: But while he thought on these things, behold, the angel of the Lord appeared unto him in a dream, saying, Joseph, thou son of David, fear not to take unto thee Mary thy wife: for that which is conceived in her is of the Holy Ghost.

24: Then Joseph being raised from sleep did as the angel of the Lord had bidden him, and took unto him his wife:

25: And knew her not till she had brought forth her firstborn son: and he called his name Jesus.

🎵 **"Joseph Dearest, Joseph Mine" (melody can be found online)**

"Joseph dearest, Joseph mine,

Help me cradle the Child divine.

God reward thee and all that's thine,

In paradise," so prays the mother Mary.

Chorus

He came among us at Christmas time,

At Christmas time in Bethlehem.

Men shall bring Him from far and wide,

Love's diadem

Jesus, Jesus;

Lo, he comes and loves and saves and frees us.

Can God Trust Me to Do His Work?

The story of Joseph is found in the account of Matthew. From Matthew's words, we learn that Mary were Joseph are espoused (a formal engagement to be married) when Mary told Joseph that she was carrying Jesus. Rather than be upset and publicly shame Mary, Joseph showed mercy and compassion and planned to end the engagement privately. While he was contemplating this, an angel appeared to him in a dream, telling him that the child was conceived of the Holy Ghost. Joseph then put aside all concerns for himself and his reputation and married Mary. Imagine the amount of trust God had in Joseph to raise His Son? Joseph took care of Mary and the baby Jesus. Joseph, like the Savior, is an example of forgiveness and mercy. We can take courage in Joseph's example when we are asked to do hard things— things that don't seem wise or may even cause others to mock us. When we listen to God with a willing and loving heart, He can heal us and help us to do His will.

Love You, Dad

Share what you love about your father or another father-like person who has influenced your life and your family. Ask the children to list all the things they think a father does, and have them draw a picture or tell a story of a special time that they spent with their dad (see "I love you, Dad" page 21). Compile all the pictures and stories together to create a book for a beloved father or grandfather in your life. If you don't live near grandparents, have the kids compose a list of questions or a song they can sing together. Make arrangements to call or video chat with a grandfather to ask questions or sing a favorite song to him.

Which Door?

Supplies needed: several copies (at least ten to fifteen) of the stable, one copy each of the Mary and Joseph and baby Jesus scripture cards, adhesive tape or sticky-tack removable adhesive putty, small treat

We assume that Mary and Joseph must have knocked on many doors on their journey into Bethlehem. Make several copies of the "Stable" scripture card (see page XXIII). Think of all the doors in your home—doors to closets, rooms, cabinets, and so on. Using the scripture cards, tape one card on the inside of several of the doors or cabinets in your home. Hide the Mary, Joseph, and baby Jesus cards randomly inside of doors around the house rather than close together. If you want to distinguish which doors are part of the game and which are not, you will want to mark those doors by tying a bow on the knob or around the door itself. Find a central gathering spot, and have family members share something they can do to make a place for Jesus in their hearts or in your home. For very young children, you will want to explain that this means thinking of things they can do to be kind and loving to others. Each person who shares gets a chance to search two doors, and *only* two doors at a time. For example, say your child offers that he can make room for Jesus by being kind to his brother. He would go to one door, open it, and see what picture is on the inside. He then chooses a second door and opens it to see what picture is on the inside of this door. If one of the two doors has a picture of Mary, Joseph, or baby Jesus, that child brings the picture back and is awarded a small token or treat. All family members play simultaneously, and everyone returns to the family meeting spot after searching two doors. If none are found, the game begins again. If all three Mary, Joseph, and baby Jesus cards are found, then all the cards are hidden again and the game starts over.

Joseph the Carpenter

In many Christian traditions, Joseph is known as the patron saint of the worker. In Matthew 13:55, Joseph is identified as a carpenter, although the word could be more generally translated as a "craftsman." Take this opportunity for the father in your home to teach or share a special skill—maybe one that the kids don't get to see him do often. Take a tour of where dad works or have some fun sharing a hobby or talent or do a small maintenance job with dad. Keep it simple and child-centered (they may be more interested in the snack machine than what he actually does). This is a time to spend as a family recognizing the important person that their father is in their lives.

Joseph's Workshop

Supplies needed: tree branches or wood cut to dimensions given on instructions, one-inch nails, wood glue, two screws, drill, screwdriver, hammer, tape measure, hand or table saw, paint or stain, Styrofoam blocks, golf tees (optional)

Download simple project plans for a small wooden bench or box, or use the following instructions to build a small, rustic manger. Instructions are given for using twigs or tree branches, but you could do an easier project by using craft sticks or twigs glued to a cardboard box. For young hands, have fun pounding "nails" (golf tees) into "boards" (Styrofoam blocks).

Rustic Twig Manger Project Plans

Supplies needed: sticks and twigs, hand saw, hot glue, twine, one-inch brads, hammer

1. Cut four sticks (about one-half to one inch in diameter) twelve inches in length.

To make the legs of the manger, cross two sticks to make an X. Glue or nail the two twigs together and wrap with twine. Repeat with the other two sticks so that the two Xs match each other.

2. Cut three sticks (about one-half to one inch in diameter) twelve inches in length.

Stand the two X legs up, and lay a twelve-inch stick in the crook of both legs. Glue or nail in place and wrap with twine.

Glue or nail a second stick (twelve inches in length) one inch below the top of the legs as shown. Wrap in twine and repeat on the other side.

3. Cut several sticks (about one-half to one inch in diameter) about six inches in length.

Lay the manger on its side, and glue or nail a six-inch stick to the middle stick and the top stick on one side. Wrap with twine. Lay the manger on the other side and repeat with a second stick. Continue to alternate sides until both sides are lined with twigs.

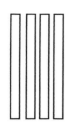

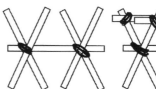
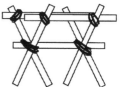

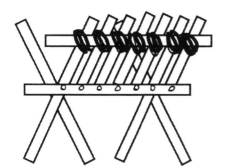

4. Fill your manger with straw or hay, and place it in a prominent spot. Add a swaddled baby doll, or display your nativity inside the completed manger.

A smaller version of this project can be made by reducing the measurements proportionally.

 Do you know of an elderly person living in your neighborhood who could use some help around the house, a kind word, or some company? Make an appointment to stop in for a visit, or extend an offer for dinner at your house. If not, arrange to visit an assisted living center and bring treats to share, if that is allowed.

"I Love You, Dad" Coloring Page

I love you!

Day 5: Donkey

Add the donkey to the nativity scene.

 Galatians 6:2 Bear ye one another's burdens, and so fulfil the law of Christ.

 "Little Donkey" (melody can be found online)

Little donkey, little donkey on the dusty road,

Got to keep on plodding onwards with your precious load.

Been a long time, little donkey, through the winter's night.

Don't give up now, little donkey,

Bethlehem's in sight.

Little donkey, little donkey, had a heavy day;

Little donkey, carry Mary safely on her way.

Little donkey, little donkey, journey's end is near;

There are Wise Men waiting for a sign to bring them here.

Strengthen My Back to Carry My Burden

While there is no scriptural mention of a donkey in the Nativity story, their use was historically widespread and common. It would make sense that Mary and Joseph traveled to Bethlehem from Nazareth with Mary, who was expecting a baby at any time, riding on a donkey. Additionally, the prophecy that the Messiah would come riding in on a donkey (see Zechariah 9:9) may be an additional reason that the donkey is placed in this story. While this prophecy was of His triumphal return before the Crucifixion, it is easy to see how it might also be assimilated into this story.

The donkey doesn't have a beautiful voice. He was probably not called upon to herald in the birth of the baby with his braying. His broad face and long ears are not necessarily beautiful to look at, and he certainly doesn't carry an air of nobility about him. Donkeys are strong, slow, stubborn, methodical, and useful. Jesus also was not known for His beauty (see Isaiah 53:2) but for His acts of service. Like the donkey, He spent His days serving the weak and underprivileged and carrying and lifting the burdens of those who were worn and weary. We can pray for the Lord to strengthen our backs to help carry the burdens of others and then be looking for those opportunities to manifest themselves. Like the donkey, we can be strong, stubborn, methodical, and useful in our service and in our belief in the Savior as we share His grace with others this season.

 ## Donkey Rides

Supplies needed: shallow bowls, family's favorite treat, blanket

For moms and dads, saddle up and take the kids on a "donkey ride." Let the little rider be your guide by giving you directions on where to go and how to get there, whether it be fast, slow, bumpy, or smooth. Let everyone enjoy a nice bowl of "special donkey hay" at the end of the ride. This could be any treat of your choosing. Just pour it into a shallow bowl or pan for each person, and let everyone (donkeys and riders alike) eat hands-free from the bowl. If your back isn't up to multiple donkey rides, an alternative is to give your kids a ride around the house on a blanket. Lay a blanket on the floor, and have a child sit in the middle of the blanket. Start out slowly so you don't tip your master over, and then gently pull the child around the house by tugging on one corner of the blanket.

Donkey Kicks

When it needs to defend itself, the donkey will use its powerful legs to kick. To do a donkey kick, crouch down on the floor so that both hands and feet are in contact with the floor. (You can also position your knees on the floor if you need.) Lean slightly forward on your arms and push your back legs out and up into the air, and then bring them back underneath you and land on all fours to complete one kick. Make a donkey hat for everyone (see donkey hat instructions in the "Nativity Dress-Up" section, page 64). Have everyone sit in a circle and choose one donkey to roll a die. Whatever number is rolled, that donkey should then do that number of donkey kicks. (Braying is optional.) Continue rolling and braying until everyone is tuckered out. You can vary the game by having the person who rolled the die choose the donkey to do the appropriate number of kicks. If your kids are savvy enough, they may soon learn the fun of piling the number of kicks on mom or dad and watch them kick themselves to exhaustion!

Donkey Sings

A popular children's Christmas song says, "Sweetly sings the donkey at the break of day, if you listen carefully, you will hear him say: HE-HAW, HE-HAW, HE-HAW, HE-HAW, HE-HAW." Contrary to the song, there are few people who would agree that a donkey sings sweetly. Pull up an audio or video file of a donkey braying online to illustrate this point. Nevertheless, the donkey is probably all heart when he does sing! In your best donkey voices, sing your favorite Christmas song, using donkey noises only—no words. The best singer gets to wear the donkey hat (see the "Nativity Dress-Up" section on page 64) for suggestions on making a donkey hat.

Variation: The song goes on to tell that the sheep and the calf also sang sweetly in their native languages. Think of other animals that might also have been at the stable that we don't traditionally use in our Nativity narrative (or make a list of your favorite animals). Make a copy of several different animals, and tape them to craft sticks. Decide what each might say, and sing the song again, this time holding up the one animal at a time to indicate which animal voice you will be singing with.

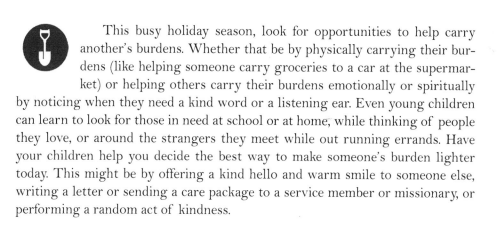

This busy holiday season, look for opportunities to help carry another's burdens. Whether that be by physically carrying their burdens (like helping someone carry groceries to a car at the supermarket) or helping others carry their burdens emotionally or spiritually by noticing when they need a kind word or a listening ear. Even young children can learn to look for those in need at school or at home, while thinking of people they love, or around the strangers they meet while out running errands. Have your children help you decide the best way to make someone's burden lighter today. This might be by offering a kind hello and warm smile to someone else, writing a letter or sending a care package to a service member or missionary, or performing a random act of kindness.

Day 6: Shepherd

Add the shepherd to the nativity scene.

Luke 2:8-18

8: And there were in the same country shepherds abiding in the field, keeping watch over their flock by night.

16: And they came with haste, and found Mary, and Joseph, and the babe lying in a manger.

17: And when they had seen it, they made known abroad the saying which was told them concerning this child.

18: And all they that heard it wondered at those things which were told them by the shepherds.

"While Shepherds Watched Their Flocks" (melody can be found online)

While shepherds watched

their flocks by night,

all seated on the ground,

The angel of the lord came down,

And Glory shone around.

"Fear not," said he,

For mighty dread had seized their troubled minds;

"Glad tidings of great joy I bring

To you and all mankind."

Am I Quick to Respond to God?

Shepherds are the people in charge of guiding and protecting flocks of sheep. Shepherds use crooks—long sticks with a hook on the end—to look for danger in unseen places, to rescue a fallen lamb, for balance when walking over difficult terrain, and for defense against predators. Because shepherds spend so much time with their sheep, they "know" their sheep, and the sheep "know" their shepherd.

As the angel approached the shepherds in the Nativity story, the shepherds were frightened, but soon the angel soothed their worries by announcing the birth of the baby Jesus. Like the Wise Men, they must have known the prophecies of the Savior's birth because they immediately dropped everything and went and found the babe. They didn't stop to buy gifts on the way, and the account doesn't tell of elaborate plans and preparations. They simply got up and went. Jesus often referred to Himself as the Good Shepherd (John 10:14–15). He watches over us, and helps us be mindful of rocky hills and dangerous predators, and He pulls us in close when we start to wander. He knows His sheep and simply asks us to know Him by humbly following His voice.

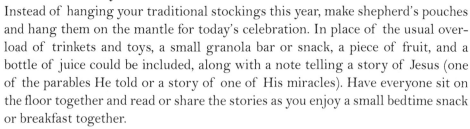

Like the shepherds, how quick are we do go and do what God wants us to do? How often are we humble enough to trust God's message for us? How anxious are we to do God's work?

Shepherd's Pouch

Shepherds live a nomadic life, following the flocks of sheep from one grazing pasture to another. A pouch or bag they could drape over their shoulders was useful to carry food or other small items. Instead of hanging your traditional stockings this year, make shepherd's pouches and hang them on the mantle for today's celebration. In place of the usual over-load of trinkets and toys, a small granola bar or snack, a piece of fruit, and a bottle of juice could be included, along with a note telling a story of Jesus (one of the parables He told or a story of one of His miracles). Have everyone sit on the floor together and read or share the stories as you enjoy a small bedtime snack or breakfast together.

Shepherd's Pouch Instructions

Supplies needed: small scraps of burlap, yarn, needle, thread or hot glue gun, scissors, rope, markers or paint

1. Cut the fabric so you have two nine-by-nine-inch pieces of burlap. Lay the two pieces on top of one another and hand stitch using yarn or thread. Sew or glue the two pieces together about one inch from the edges. Sew both sides and the bottom only, leaving the top edge open. You can easily fray the edges of the burlap by pulling the loose threads as shown.

2. Using scissors, pierce two holes about one inch from the top of both sides of the bag you have sewn. Thread the rope through the holes, adjust the length to fit over the shoulder of your child, and cut and knot the rope on each end.

3. Decorate, if desired, with markers or paint.

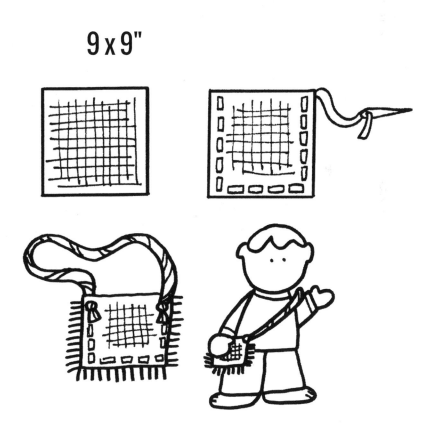

9 x 9"

Shepherd's Picnic

When the shepherds were out in the pastures watching their flocks, they ate and slept wherever the sheep were grazing. Bundle up and take a picnic lunch to a grassy park or field. If the weather is inclement, lay a blanket out on the floor and have your meal indoors. Turn out the lights and eat by lantern or candlelight.

Luke 2 tells us that after the shepherds visited the babe in the manger, they returned and told everyone what they saw. Share your favorite memories of Christmases past as you share your meal. Be sure to write down or record the stories on video as a compilation of family memories.

Shepherd's Crook

Supplies needed: small stuffed animals, small loops such as diving rings (optional), large ornamental candy cane or newspapers, wire coat hangers, duct tape

Purchase a large ornamental candy cane or create your own shepherd's crook. This can be done by rolling up newspapers into a long tube. Place a straightened wire hanger down through the middle, and then wrap the length of newspapers in tape. Bend the end with the wire into a crook. (Or if you want to create a really simple crook, simply straighten the wire hanger and bend the end into a crook.) Make one for each member of the family.

Place several stuffed animals on one end of the room. Divide into teams and designate a "safe pasture" for each team. At the signal, each shepherd uses his or her crook to get the stuffed animal to the team pasture on the opposite side of the room. The shepherds take turns gathering the animals into their pastures. The team that gets the most stuffed animals across the room into their pasture wins. You can add another challenge to the game by allowing the shepherds to steal the animals from the other team's flock with their crooks.

Variation: Use the shepherd's crooks to move small rings or hoops from one location to another around the house. You can use small plastic hoops, like diving rings for pool play, or make your own using the newspaper and tape technique detailed above. Start with a hoop on the ground and have the first person pick it up with the hook and carefully carry it and hook it around a door knob or other protrusion (like a finial on the stairs, a chair leg, and so on). The next family member must use his or her crook to remove the ring and move it to a new location. Devise a course and assign points to each location based on difficulty. Work in teams to see who can complete the course the fastest.

Much like how the shepherds spent their days taking care of animals, you can also find a way to help out God's creatures. Check with your local animal shelter for current needs. Many accept small blankets that can easily be made from scraps of fleece or towels that the animals can use for bedding. Organize your neighborhood, school, or church community to gather supplies or funds to purchase food or shelter for an animal of your choosing.

Day 7: Sheep

Add the sheep to the nativity scene.

 John 10:27 My sheep hear my voice, and I know them, and they follow me.

 "What Can I Give Him?" (melody can be found online)

What can I give Him, as small as I am?

If I were a shepherd, I'd give Him a lamb,

If I were a wise man, I'd do my part,

I know what I'll give Him,

I'll give Him my heart.

What can I give Him to show Him my Love?

The stars smile on Him and twinkle above.

They sing me a song that shines in the dark.

I know what I'll give Him, I'll give Him my heart.

I know what I'll give Him, I'll give Him my heart.

Am I Willing to Follow the Good Shepherd?

Sheep have good hearing and excellent peripheral vision (they can see behind their own ears without turning around). They are skittish about shadows and will seek light whenever possible. They have a natural tendency to follow their shepherd and are known to be able to recognize their master by his voice. The Savior, like a lamb, was meek and humble to do His father's will.

Like the sheep in the Nativity story, we should also be able to hear and recognize the Good Shepherd's voice (John 10:3–4). We should come quickly when He calls and follow Him to safe passages and greener pastures.

Hide-and-Go-Sheep

Choose a small sheep from a nativity set (you may want to purchase a small stuffed animal or print out a picture of a sheep or the "Hide-and-Go-Sheep" activity cards [see page 35] for this activity). Hide the sheep somewhere in the house. He might be perched on the mantle or peeking out of the cereal box. The first person to find it gets to hide it for the next round.

Variation: Print several copies of the "Hide-and-Go-Sheep" activity cards (see page 35). Hide these copies around the house. At a given signal, family members head out to find as many sheep as they can. The person who returns with the most sheep gets a special prize.

Variation: Print several copies of the "Hide-and-Go-Sheep" activity cards (see page 35). Hide these copies around the house. Beginning with one sheep clue, leave a note leading to where the next sheep is hidden. You may choose to also include a small activity or task to be performed at each hiding place, such as, "Sheep give their wool to make woolen socks. See how many socks you can correctly match and fold within sixty seconds of finding this sheep," or, "Call Grandma and sing her your favorite Christmas carol using your best sheep voice (no human words). Hang up and leave her guessing as to which of her favorite little lambs made the call."

Variation: Choose a small sheep from a nativity set. (You may want to purchase a small stuffed animal or print out a picture of a sheep or make a copy of the "Hide-and-Go-Sheep" activity cards [see page 35] for this activity.) Hide the sheep somewhere in the house or take the little sheep with you while running errands. Take a picture of the sheep in several different locations (for example at your favorite fast food restaurant), but include only a small sample of that location or that location's sign as background in the picture. See who can correctly identify where each sheep is hiding. Extend the game by having one parent set out before the rest of the family. Take a picture of the sheep at a location and text the pictures to the family left behind. Leave a clue "Hide-and-Go-Sheep" activity card (see page 35) to find. Once it is found, the family texts the first parent, who sends the new clue.

The Sheep Hear My Voice

(Make sure to play this game in a large open area devoid of obstacles and potentially hazardous situations.) Choose two family members to be "the shepherds." All other family members are to be sheep and are assigned to a shepherd. The sheep are blindfolded while the shepherds scramble away to another part of the room and call to their sheep. The sheep then move as quickly as possible to find their shepherd. Once the sheep have all gathered together, the shepherd may lead them around the room by calling for them to follow.

 Sheep give their cozy wool so that we can make clothing and other useful items. Give a gift of comfort by making or donating a blanket or sheets to a homeless shelter, adult assisted living center, or hospital. (Be sure to check with the shelter or hospital for special donation guidelines.) Or perhaps you might know of someone in your neighborhood or church congregation who would appreciate a warm and anonymous woolen hug this season.

Use these sheep cards for writing "Hide-and-Go- Sheep" clues, or use them to make cards for a matching game.

Day 8: Angel

Add the angel to the nativity scene.

📖 Luke 2:10 And the angel said unto them, Fear not: for, behold, I bring you good tidings of great joy, which shall be to all people.

13: And suddenly there was with the angel a multitude of the heavenly host praising God, and saying,

14: Glory to God in the highest, and on earth peace, good will toward men.

🎵 "Angels We Have Heard on High" (melody can be found online)

Angels we have heard on high
Sweetly singing o'er the plains,
And the mountains in reply
Echoing their joyous strains.
Gloria, in excelsis Deo
Gloria, in excelsis Deo

💬 ## Would I Have Heard the Angels Sing?

While the angel who appeared to the shepherds in the fields gets a lot of the attention, there are actually three other angel appearances in the Nativity story. The first angel appears at the beginning of the story, when the angel Gabriel came to Mary to tell her of God's plan for her (Luke 1:26–38). The second angel appearance is when the angel of the Lord visited Joseph to tell him of Mary's condition and to announce that the baby would be Jesus (Matthew 1:20–24). The third angel appearance was to the shepherds, and the fourth was to Joseph again after the Wise Men came. This angel warned Joseph to flee out of Bethlehem.

Angels are often described as childlike winged creatures who are white-robed and adorned with golden halos. While we may not know exactly what an angel looks like, we can assume that they are beings of extraordinary light. They are described as having the glory of the Lord shining about them. Whenever God has an important message to share with people in the scriptures, He often sends an angel to be the messenger.

After the angel announced the Savior's birth to the shepherds, there was a multitude of heavenly hosts praising God. It must have been an amazing and jubilant scene. Why didn't others see the heavenly hosts and hear the angles sing? How often do I make a joyful noise? How does God reveal Himself to you? Am I one to bring good tidings to someone in the dark of night who needs to hear God's word? We can be the angelic means by which someone feels and knows of God's love by being a messenger of His good works.

Make a Joyful Noise

Supplies needed: various toy instruments (bells, triangles, tambourines, kazoos, and so on), pots, pans, various recyclables (milk jugs or empty boxes)

Use the musical supplies you have gathered to experiment with music and make a joyful noise. You can use typical musical instruments or make instruments out of found objects such as buckets, boxes, tin cans, silverware, and so on. You can drum, tap, or blow on just about anything. Use your instruments to accompany you as you sing your favorite Christmas carols. There are many online resources for building a wide variety of simple, kid-friendly instruments.

Variation: Make up your own angel songs by creating new words and music. You can make up new words to a familiar tune (such as "Twinkle, Twinkle, Little Star") or make up your own tune. Be sure to record it so you can remember it the next time you want to make a joyful noise.

Angel Wings

Supplies needed: paper plates (the plain ones with the ribbed edges), glue, yarn or ribbon, scissors, markers or crayons (optional)

Create your own angel wings with paper plates. Cut one full paper plate in half to create a base. Cut individual "feathers" by separating the ribbed edges of the paper plates from the smooth centers. Cut the feathers as shown so that each feather is approximately six inches long and tapered at the edges. Glue the feathers all over the two halved sections to create two separate wings. Glue these two wing sections to the middle of a single paper plate, adjusting the angle as shown so the bottom of the wings fan out and making sure that the outside edge of the single plate is separate from the wings. Once the glue has dried, decorate or color your angel wings if desired using crayons, markers, or other craft items. Poke two holes through the plate on the underside plate of the wings as shown. Using a length of ribbon or yarn, lace the ribbon through the top hole on one side, and then again through the hole on the other side. Take the ribbon ends over each shoulder and around the back. Cross the ribbon in the back, and bring it back around to the front. Tie the ribbon in a bow around the waist.

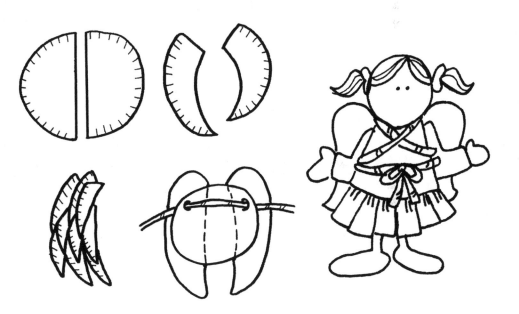

Halo Tossing

Supplies needed: nine copies of the "Shepherd" scripture card (see page XXXIII), gold tinsel, gold spray paint (optional), glue, paper plate, painter's tape

Make a nine-by-nine-foot grid on the floor with painter's tape so that each square is one square foot. Write the numbers one, three, and five on the shepherd cards, and set them randomly in the center of each square in the grid.

Make a "halo" for each child by cutting the center out of a paper plate, leaving the outside ring intact. Glue a length of the gold tinsel around the ring, or color the ring gold with spray paint.

Have the family take turns standing outside the grid (how far each family member should stand will be determined by their age or skill level). Take turns tossing your halo into the center of the grid. Collect the shepherd that your halo lands on. Once all the shepherds have been "haloed," each person tallies up their total number of points, the cards are returned to the grid, and play begins again. You can determine the prize for the highest number of points, the most cards collected, and so on.

Angel Messages

Make several copies of the "Angel" scripture card (see page XXXV). Trim around the edges of the cards, and have the family color or decorate the cards as desired. On the back of each card, write a message of encouragement, love, or hope. You can use inspirational messages or scriptures about the Savior. Take the cards and place them randomly about your community. You might stick one in a mailbox or on a doorstep. You might leave others on windshields in a parking lot. Others could be tucked on subway or bus seats or left at the table of a fast food restaurant. Have your children help you think of creative places to leave these little angel messages that may bring hope or joy to an unsuspecting stranger.

Find an "angel" tree in your community, and participate by having your family choose one of the kids on the tree. Spend time as a family shopping for the item listed. Make a copy of the "Angel" scripture card and write a brief note on the back highlighting how much you have loved shopping for this child and are grateful for the opportunity to do so. Slip the angel message inside the packaging so the recipient receives this extra note of love and encouragement when he or she opens the gift.

Day 9: Star

Add the star to the nativity scene.

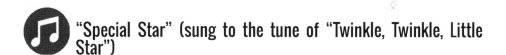 ## Matthew 2:9-10

9: When they had heard the king, they departed; and, lo, the star, which they saw in the east, went before them, till it came and stood over where the young child was.

10: When they saw the star, they rejoiced with exceeding great joy.

"Special Star" (sung to the tune of "Twinkle, Twinkle, Little Star")

Twinkle, twinkle, special star

How I wonder what you are

Guiding Wise Men on their way

To manger where the baby lay

Twinkle, twinkle, special star

How I wonder what you are

Am I Looking for a Star and Coming to Adore?

The star is an integral part of the Nativity story because it is the star that marked the spot for the Wise Men to find the babe. While it is not found in the Bible, other written works must have prophesied of the star's importance, because the Wise Men knew of it and knew to follow it. The star is symbolic of light in the darkness, showing us the way to the Savior. While looking for evidences to the elements in the Nativity story, some have wondered if this star that appeared brighter than the others and also moved in the sky might have been an astronomical event. We don't know for sure what caused this star of Bethlehem to have peculiar qualities, but we can ask ourselves, Am I looking for a star, and am I coming to adore the baby who would grow up to become the Savior? Are we looking for signs that God is in our lives, and (in the process) drawing closer to the Savior? Are we looking for signs that God is in our lives, or are we merely asking to see what is already there if we will look?

Jesus has told us that He is the Light of the World and that when we follow Him, we will not walk in darkness (see John 8:12). In John 1:5, we are told that "light shineth in darkness; and the darkness comprehendeed it not." Much like how the darkness can't overcome a candle in the night, the Light of the Savior can always dispel the dark. During this season of many, many lights, it is the contrast between the light and the dark that makes the light so beautiful. And it is the contrast of the Savior's light against all that is dark that makes His light so meaningful.

 ## Lights, Lights Everywhere

Tonight is a good night to make an excursion to go see the lights of Christmas. Enjoy some hot chocolate and a treat as you peruse the neighborhood or enjoy a commercially produced production of lights. Be sure to listen to and sing Christmas carols as you explore the lights of your city.

When you arrive home, set out a string of twinkle lights in your yard or across the ceiling in your child's room. If possible, find a single star light and hang it amongst the other twinkle lights. Before going to bed, sing a song about the star or other favorite carol (see "Special Star" song, or choose another favorite, such as "O Holy Night" or "Silent Night").

Candle in the Park

Bundle up the family for some after-dark fun in the park. (You can adapt this to a darkened area indoors if the weather is inclement.) Choose one person to be the star, and give them a flashlight. While the rest of the family counts to one hundred while covering their eyes, the "star" runs and hides somewhere in the park, making sure that their flashlight is on. After counting to one hundred, the rest of the family disburses to find the star. Once they have found it, they should sit with the star until all the family members have found it. A new star is chosen, and the game continues. Have some hot chocolate or cider ready to warm everyone up when you finish your game and are headed for home.

Variation: Play in the park, or turn off all the lights in the house (keep a few small lamps or night lights on for ambient light). Choose one area or room to be the starting place and another area or room in another part of the house to be the finishing place. Have one person with the flashlight hide somewhere in the house. As members try to silently move from one place to the other, the person with the flashlight tries to "catch" them with the light as they pass by.

Starlight Caroling

Supplies needed: starlight candleholder (hammer, nails, wire, clean metal can, small candle), starlight flashlight (flashlight, light-colored or transparent heavy plastic folders, scissors, heavy-duty clear tape)

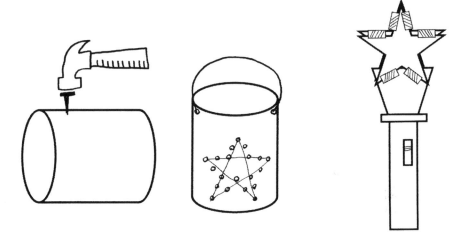

Weather permitting, light a candle or make a starlight lantern or starlight flashlight, and go for a walk through the neighborhood. Pick a few homes of neighbors and sing to them by candlelight on the porch.

Commercial candleholders can be purchased online. You can also make your own starlight lantern by punching nails into a tin can to make a starlight candleholder. Using a clean, empty can, fill it with water and put it in the freezer. Once the ice is solid, punch holes as desired by tapping a nail through the can into the ice. (The ice will help the can hold its shape as you pound the nails into it.) You can draw a design or star shape on the can and then punch holes at one-half-inch intervals along the edges. Punch two holes on opposite sides of the can near the top, and string a length of wire through both holes to create a handle. Place a tea light or small candle inside, and once lit, your punched design will light up from within the lantern.

To make a starlight flashlight, cut two star shapes out of a heavy yellow, white, or clear plastic folder. (Use light-colored, or transparent folders for best results.) Tape the bottom points of one star to the top of a flashlight, and repeat on the other side. Using a clear or transparent piece of tape, tape the other three points to one another so your star wraps over the top of the flashlight. Your star will glow when you turn on your flashlight.

Star Tag

Supplies needed: flashlight, star stickers or stamp with washable ink

Clear a large room of furniture and other obstacles by pushing them up against a wall. (You may want to have some ambient light in the room by turn-ing on a light in another room that can filter in and give just enough light to see yet still keep the room dark.) One person is chosen to be "it." They are given a flashlight, and when they say "go," all other family members must dash (or sneak) from one end of the room to the other, trying not to get tagged by the "starlight." The person who is it must turn the light on and off to tag someone; they cannot constantly have the beam on searching for someone to tag. Anyone who gets tagged must sit out until everyone has made it to the other side of the room. If you got tagged, you get a star sticker to show that you've been "starstruck," and play begins again with a new person flashing the light.

Involve your neighborhood in a gift of service. Write a small note expressing your appreciation for the gift of the light of the Savior in your life (or a similar message of hope). You can use the "'Light in the Darkness' Donation Request Note" (page 47), if desired, or create one of your own. In your note, include the following information:

- your plan to gather donations to provide light for others by supporting a local charity that helps pay utility bills for elderly and fixed-income homes
- what kinds of donations will be accepted (will you accept cash or checks or electronic transfers?)
- a suggested donation amount
- what day or time you will be collecting donations
- where to place the candle so you can see it from the outside the home

Purchase several small battery-operated candles and batteries. Tie the note to the candle, and deliver one to each household in your neighborhood or along your street. Encourage each family to light their candle and place it in the window on a specific night to let you know that they plan to donate. Then, as you take a starlit walk through your neighborhood, look for burning candles and stop to pick up the donations. Deliver the donation as a family, and be sure to send a thank-you card to each family who donates. (You can use the "Bethlehem Star" scripture card, page XXXVII, for thank-you notes after the donations have been made.)

"A Light in the Darkness" Donation Request Note

Our family is so grateful for the light of the Savior in our lives. At this time of the year, we want to share light with others, and we hope you'll consider joining us. On _____ , we will be walking through the neighborhood to gather donations to provide light for others by supporting _____ , a local charity that helps pay utility bills for elderly and fixed-income homes in our community. No set amount is required to participate; any gift will be accepted, although a suggested donation amount might be _____. We will accept [cash, checks, or electronic transfers].

If you would like to participate with us, please light this candle on the night of _____ and place it in your window or on your porch so we can see it. We will stop by to collect your donation and add it to others from the neighborhood. If you will not be at home but would like to contribute anyway, please contact us at _____.

Thank you!

Day 10: Camel

Add the camel to the nativity scene.

 Matthew 24:13 He that shall endure unto the end, the same shall be saved.

 "Three Little Camels" (sung to the tune of "The First Noel")

The first little camel walked over the sand

Over hills and mountains to a faraway land

The kings pressed on, into the dark night

To follow the star and it's Holy light

The second little camel carried gifts so rare

Over rivers and valleys they were heavy to bear

The kings pressed on, long into the dark night

To follow the star and it's Holy light.

The third little camel walked beside each King

And heard stories of the baby, great joy would He bring

The kings pressed on, long into the dark night

To follow the star and it's Holy light

Three camels small, kings and gifts they did bring

And they knelt down in awe when they found the small king.

Am I Willing to Allow Jesus to Love Me in Spite of My Knobby Knees?

Although the camel is never mentioned in the scriptural accounts of the Nativity, it is often included in the nativity *crèche* because it is assumed that would have been the customary way to travel. Stubborn and hard to train, camels require a lot of effort to make them into working animals. But once trained, they are loyal and submissive to their master.

Camels are certainly not beautiful animals by most standards. They have long knobby knees, tufts of matted hair, large nostrils, and they spit when threatened. But it is those odd features that perfectly equip the camel to withstand long workdays without water and harsh temperatures. How beautiful it is that the Savior loves us in spite of our knobby knees and stubborn streaks? He values us for our willingness to train our hearts to Him. How comforting to know that He created us with the characteristics and temperaments to thrive in whatever place we find ourselves. He is the loving Master who fits our pack to our backs for each day's journey and the one who will lift it from our backs at the end of the day (Matthew 11:30). Am I willing to allow the Savior to be my Master? Am I willing to follow Him and serve Him? Am I allowing Him to use me, in spite of my imperfections?

How to Train a Camel

Camels must go through a rigorous training process in order to be ready for service. Have everyone stand in a circle. Have one person stand in the middle of the circle as the camel trainer. The camel trainer calls out one command, such as "stand on one foot" or "move your arms." Everyone in the circle repeats the action given. Keep adding on activities until one of the "camels" fails to train correctly by stopping one or more of the activities. Have that person sit out for a rest. Play continues until there is only one camel left. Play again with the newly trained camel as the camel trainer.

Pack It

Supplies needed: blankets, pillows, stuffed animals, and other soft items

How many things can you pack on a camel's back? How far can you go? Have one person get on his or her hands and knees. Gather lots of blankets, pillows, stuffed animals, and so on, and see how many you can stack on your camel's back. Then see how far that person can travel on all fours around the house before everything falls off.

Sand and Stars

Supplies needed: large, flat container; sand; water; star-shaped cookie cutter; spoon; disposable bucket and stirring stick; plaster of Paris (found at craft supply stores); wooden skewer; craft paints

Fill a large, shallow container with sand. Pour a little water in with the sand, and stir until all the sand is damp (you shouldn't be able to see any of the water). Press the sand flat in the container, and then insert the star-shaped cookie cutter into the sand. Using a small spoon, scoop the sand from the inside of the cookie cutter, and carefully remove the cookie cutter from the sand to reveal a star-shaped impression in the sand. In a separate disposable bucket, mix plaster of Paris and water according to package directions. Pour the plaster into the star mold, and use the wooden skewer to make a small hole in one of the star's points. Allow the plaster to dry completely. Remove and paint as desired. Using craft paints, decorate your star in any way you wish. Place a short length of string or ribbon through the hole and hang it as an ornament on your tree. You can create other shapes, letters, and forms in the same way.

Make up a bag of several items, including snacks, hand wipes, hand warmers, gloves, a hat, a water bottle, small toiletry items, and so on, and deliver it with a smile to a lonely traveler who is sitting or standing on a corner, looking for help. Jesus was a great example of giving service without judgment to make someone else's journey a little easier. We can give what we can and be confident that any time we give of ourselves, we bring a little goodness into the lives of others, and we cannot keep it from ourselves. Make it a goal to provide this kind of service throughout the year.

Day 11: Wise Men

Add the Wise Men to the nativity scene.

 Matthew 2:1-2

1: Now when Jesus was born in Bethlehem of Judea in the days of Herod the king, behold, there came wise men from the east to Jerusalem,

2: saying, Where is he that is born King of the Jews? for we have seen his star in the east, and are come to worship him.

🎵 **"We Three Kings" (melody can be found online)**

We three kings of Orient are

Bearing gifts we travel afar.

Field and fountain, moor and mountain,

Following yonder star.

O star of wonder, star of night,

Star of royal beauty bright,

Westward leading, still proceeding,

Following yonder star.

💬 **What Lengths Will I Go to Seek Him?**

The Wise Men (also known as noblemen, astrologers, kings, and priests) saw the new star in the sky and set out to find the new babe. Their wisdom was evident because they knew of the new star and of the prophecies about it and then took up the task of traveling from the East to bring the Savior gifts and worship Him. While the scriptures don't give us a specific number of Wise Men who visited, there have typically been three in the nativity

crèche because there were three gifts mentioned. The gifts they brought were of gold, frankincense, and myrrh—each having a significant symbolic meaning. While extraordinary for a child, these gifts would have been ordinary and suitable to bring to a king.

The Nativity story tells us that they traveled from the East, presumably from far away, because the journey took several years to reach Jesus, who was no longer a babe when they found Him (Matthew 2:9). No doubt it was an epic endeavor and a great expense to embark on such a journey.

Jesus also brings us great gifts: our lives, His grace, and our own resurrection. Our gift to Him is our continued efforts to be thoughtful about our faith, to be willing to go to extraordinary lengths to seek Him, and to give ourselves to Him.

The "Day of the Kings" (or Epiphany) is celebrated on January 6 to commemorate the day the Wise Men arrived in Bethlehem. It is the last day of the Twelve Days of Christmas if you are celebrating it from December 25 to January 6.

Gifts of Gold

Giving gifts is a big holiday tradition. Instead of having your children give the usual gifts, consider having them give one another gifts of service this year. Encourage them to be thoughtful and give something meaningful to the person who is receiving the gift. Have your family write notes of appreciation for the gifts they have received from all their friends and family. You can use the nativity thank-you card (see page 57), or have your family create one of their own.

For older children, you can talk about what gifts you would have brought to the baby in Bethlehem and what gifts you could give Him now. Write these thoughts down on a slip of paper, and wrap it up in a box and place it under the tree. Share your Christmas gifts with one another on Christmas morning as the first gifts of Christmas.

Treasure Hunt

Supplies needed: ingredients for your family's favorite cookie recipe, small boxes or gift bags, several copies of the Wise Men gift hunt page (see page 56)

Gather all the ingredients needed to make your family's favorite batch of cookies. You may want to premeasure each item or place the container and the measuring cup or spoon inside a decorated box or gift bag. Using the copies of the Wise Man gift hunt note, write clues about where to find the next gift. You can choose to make the hunt simple by giving a direct clue like, "It is in a box in the refrigerator," or you can make the clue that requires a little deciphering like, "*Brrr!* Hurry up and find the next clue! It's really *cold* in here!"

Once you have collected all the clues, take turns adding the wrapped ingredients to make the cookies. While the cookies are baking, make thank-you notes or Christmas greeting cards for friends or neighbors. (You can use the nativity scripture cards, see pages XX–XXLIII, or make your own.) Once the cookies are out of the oven and cooled, package them and dress in your finest Wise Men fashions (see the "Nativity Dress-Up" section on page 64 for suggestions) to deliver the goodies.

Spice Art

Supplies needed: spices, cotton balls, white glue, small paper cup, paint brush, paper, gold paint marker

Myrrh and frankincense are both aromatic and are often used in creating perfumes and incense. While you may not have a stash of myrrh on hand, gather a

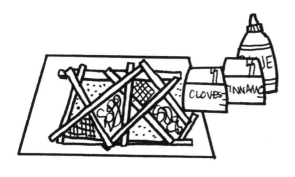

small collection of spices and extracts from your cabinet. Rub a small amount on your finger or a cotton ball (work it in well so that there are no loose particles left that can be inhaled), and let each family member sniff to see if it is a scent they like or dislike.

Create a piece of scented artwork by drawing several straight lines across the paper with the gold marker. Once it has dried, use white glue (thinned with a little bit of water so that it can be spread easily on the paper) inside one of the squares created by the gold lines you have drawn. Carefully shake or spoon a small amount of a preferred spice over the glue, and tap the paper so the excess falls off the paper. Repeat with other spices as desired. When your artwork has dried, you may want to cut it into shapes and hang it on your tree as ornaments

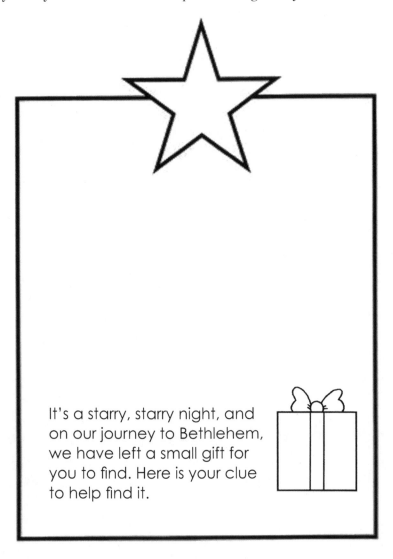

It's a starry, starry night, and on our journey to Bethlehem, we have left a small gift for you to find. Here is your clue to help find it.

Thanks!

by punching a hole in the top of each shape and lacing a short length of string through the hole.

Variation: Myrrh and frankincense can both be found as essential oils and purchased online or at a local store that sells essential oils. You may want to splurge to try out a little frankincense and myrrh as your new holiday fragrances.

This time of year, there are lots of opportunities to give gifts to organizations in need. Scout out different options in your community (Salvation Army, local charities, angel trees, and so on) that need specific items, and then take your family shopping. Talk about the person you are buying for and what your family hopes this person receives this Christmas season. (Hint: not all gifts come in a box!) Take the gift to the donation center or drive as a family. For example, in the area where we live, local TV stations operate a toy drive and have specific drop-off times and locations. Load up the car with Christmas carols and hot chocolate, and drive to the donation site. Make sure your kids get to hand over the gift to the volunteers. If there isn't an organized toy drive in your area, check with your local school or church community for suggestions of individuals who might not otherwise be remembered with a gift this year.

Day 12: Baby Jesus

Add the baby Jesus to the nativity scene.

 Luke 2:11-12

11: For unto you is born this day in the city of David a Saviour, which is Christ the Lord.

12: And this shall be a sign unto you; Ye shall find the babe wrapped in swaddling clothes, lying in a manger.

"What Child Is This?" (melody can be found online)

What child is this, who, laid to rest,

On Mary's lap is sleeping?

Whom angels greet with anthems sweet,

While shepherds watch are keeping?

This, this is Christ the King,

Whom shepherds guard and angels sing:

Haste, haste to bring Him laud,

The babe, the son of Mary.

The Baby

"For God so loved the world, that he gave his only begotten Son, that whosoever believeth in him should not perish, but have everlasting life" (John 3:16). The birth of the Savior was God's greatest gift to mankind. He is the Light in the darkness (John 12:46), the Good Shepherd (John 10:14), the way, the truth, and the life (John 14:6). He came into this life as a simple babe, who grew in grace (Luke 2:40) until He understood His father's mission. Why did He come as a baby instead the triumphal King? Did He need time to grow into what the Father sent Him to do? Maybe it was a symbol for us to see how God can take something innocent and helpless and, bit by bit, change Him into what would be His ultimate destiny. We don't know much about Jesus as a child, or what He was like as a teen or young adult, but we do know that God had great plans for Him. The reason the story of the baby is so remarkable is because of the way that He lived. We too are a work in progress for God. We too are small and weak and in need of constant nurturing, and isn't it interesting that as we strive to become like Him, we are ever more in need of His help to do just that? On this Holy Night, take a moment to reflect on all that you have read and heard and done as you have celebrated the 12-Day Nativity. Have we made more room for Him in our inn? Are we willing to drop all and go with haste to Him? Are we willing to follow the light or acknowledge that, in spite of our riches, our honors, and our knowledge (or lack thereof), we need the baby Jesus? The challenge now is to take that sacred call and extend it to the 353 other days of the year. Celebrating Christ at Christmas is a great way to honor Him, but how much more meaningful it would be if we could hold that little babe in our arms (and He us) throughout the year.

Straw for the Baby

Supplies needed: small cardboard box, glue, craft sticks or twigs, straw-colored paper

A popular holiday tradition is to make or buy a small wooden box or manger, and then have the family fill the box with hay. (See "Rustic Twig Manger Project Plans," page 18.) This is done by adding one piece of straw to the manger for each good deed or act of kindness that a family member shows throughout the day, with the intent that by Christmas Eve, the manger would be full enough with hay for the baby Jesus to sleep.

An alternative but similar activity is to gather a small box and have your children glue craft sticks or twigs onto the sides of the box to create a manger. Cut several small one-half-inch strips of yellow or straw-colored paper. Have each family member write on each strip of paper something that they are thankful for, such as a blessing from God, or a time when someone did something loving and kind for them. Share each one as you add it to the box to prepare the manger for baby Jesus.

"Gift for Him" Notes

Before the hustle and bustle of Christmas dinner or presents or all those other fun Christmas Eve traditions that you undertake, pause for a moment and make a Christmas list of gifts for the Savior. Gifts can be simple, such as, "loving my brother" or "playing nicely with the cat." Some can be gifts of self, such as, "remembering to be thankful or content." (Very young children will not be able to think so abstractly and will be prone to wanting to give the baby a doll or ball, and that is okay. The point of this activity is to try to think of others.) Gifts could include things that you believe the Savior would wish for, such as peace or that all could see themselves as His family. Place these notes in a special stocking set aside for the baby Jesus. Keep the notes from year to year as memories of years past, and read the gifts each Christmas.

Gather your "Gift for Him" notes and read and talk about the gifts and experiences that you have had with the Savior throughout this 12-Day Nativity season.

What can I give Him? If we were to ask Jesus what He wants most, I think He would want for each of us to love and take care of one another in the way He would if He could be here with us. Consider the place setting you set out on the table as you prepared to celebrate the 12-Day Nativity. Find someone in your neighborhood, church community, or a work acquaintance who would be celebrating Christmas Eve alone, and invite them to join your family for dinner and fill that empty place at the table. Encourage your guest to share stories of Christmases past and any traditions or memories that remind them about the Nativity. Send your special guest home with a small nativity as a keepsake of the evening.

Nativity Pageant

Use this outline to present your own Nativity pageant. You may want to use the "Nativity Dress-Up" section (see page 64) to decide what to wear. You will need a narrator, Joseph, Mary, a donkey, shepherds, sheep, three Wise Men, and a camel. Other props that you may want to gather include a box or cradle for the stable, a baby and small blanket, and a star. You may also want to provide a way to play music to accompany the songs. If you have enough family members or other friends or neighbors who are joining you, you can divide up the narration and songs.

Luke 2

1: And it came to pass in those days, that there went out a decree from Caesar Augustus, that all the world should be taxed.
2: (And this taxing was first made when Cyrenius was governor of Syria.)
3: And all went to be taxed, every one into his own city.
4: And Joseph also went up from Galilee, out of the city of Nazareth, into Judea, unto the city of David, which is called Bethlehem.

Enter Mary on donkey and Joseph.

Song: "O Little Town of Bethlehem"

5: To be taxed with Mary his espoused wife, being great with child.
6: And so it was, that, while they were there, the days were accomplished that she should be delivered.

Lay the baby Jesus in the manger.

Song: "Away in a Manger"

7: And she brought forth her firstborn son, and wrapped him in swaddling clothes, and laid him in a manger; because there was no room for them in the inn.
8: And there were in the same country shepherds abiding in the field, keeping watch over their flock by night.

Enter shepherds, sheep, and angel.

9: And, lo, the angel of the Lord came upon them, and the glory of the Lord shone round about them: and they were sore afraid.

10: And the angel said unto them, Fear not: for, behold, I bring you good tidings of great joy, which shall be to all people.

11: For unto you is born this day in the city of David a Saviour, which is Christ the Lord.

12: And this shall be a sign unto you; Ye shall find the babe wrapped in swaddling clothes, lying in a manger.

13: And suddenly there was with the angel a multitude of the heavenly host praising God, and saying,

14: Glory to God in the highest, and on earth peace, good will toward men.

 Song: "Hark the Herald Angels Sing"

 15: And it came to pass, as the angels were gone away from them into heaven, the shepherds said one to another, Let us now go even unto Bethlehem, and see this thing which is come to pass, which the Lord hath made known unto us.

16: And they came with haste, and found Mary, and Joseph, and the babe lying in a manger.

Enter Wise Men and camel.

Song: "We Three Kings"

Matthew 2

 1: Now when Jesus was born in Bethlehem of Judea in the days of Herod the king, behold, there came wise men from the east to Jerusalem,

2: Saying, Where is he that is born King of the Jews? For we have seen his star in the east, and are come to worship him.

9: When they had heard the king, they departed; and, lo, the star, which they saw in the east, went before them, till it came and stood over where the young child was.

10: When they saw the star, they rejoiced with exceeding great joy.

11: And when they were come into the house, they saw the young child with Mary his mother, and fell down, and worshipped him: and when they had opened their treasures, they presented unto him gifts; gold, and frankincense, and myrrh.

 Song: "Silent Night"

Nativity Dress-Up

If you sew a lot, there are lots of ornate patterns that can be purchased for nativity costumes. If you prefer a no-sew option, use the following instructions to create your own collection of nativity dress-ups or costumes. Instructions are given for child- and adult-sized costumes. Watch Halloween clearance sales for items such as wigs and beards. Keep each costume in a separate bag, labeled with the character's name, and keep all of them together in one box or bin so they are always ready when you need them. Instructions are given for a basic costume. You may choose to embellish with decorative elements or other accessories as desired.

Here are a few other props or materials you may need:

- manger
- baby Jesus
- a star (this could be hung by a string from a dowel and carried by the Wise Men)
- staffs for the shepherds
- gifts for the Wise Men
- safety pins and balloons (needed for last-minute alterations and for the animals' costumes)

Supplies Needed: iron, scissors, tape measure, sewing machine or needle and thread, hot blue gun and glue, stitch witchery, pins

Project hints: If the fabric you have purchased frays (the edges start to separate), and you choose not to sew your nativity costumes, here is a no-sew option that will keep the edges from fraying. Apply Fray Check (a liquid seam sealant available wherever sewing supplies are sold) to the edges. After the Fray Check has dried, fold the edge of the fabric over a half inch, and press with an iron. Use Stitch Witchery (a product that bonds seams together when ironed) or run a bead of hot glue along the edge of the fabric and fold the edge at the crease and glue the edge to the body of the fabric. This will give you a finished edge even if you aren't handy with a sewing machine.

Tunic (Mary, Joseph, shepherds, angel, and Wise Men)

Supplies needed: fabric, scissors, measuring tape, dinner or salad plate, Fray Check (can be purchased wherever sewing supplies are sold), iron, hot glue

Fabrics: Purchase separate fabrics for each character. Often, scraps or bargain bins are great places to find the fabric you want. Inexpensive sheets (flat) or clearance tablecloths are also good sources for fabric. Knit (stretchy) fabric will not fray on the edges and will be easier to construct as a result. Consider using earthy or rustic fabrics or tones for Mary, Joseph, and the shepherds. Purchase white for the angel and sheep, gray for the donkey, brown for the camel, and bright jewel tones for the kings. Consider patterns and textures when you buy to add extra visual interest. Measurements are provided for child, youth, and adult costumes. Tunic length can be easily adjusted by tying a sash or belt around the waist, and then pulling the tunic up until the desired length is met. This will create a blousing effect but will allow you to adjust the tunic to any desired length.

Child Tunic (fits average-sized child, six years and under): One yard of fabric. Cut one piece eighteen by thirty-six inches.

Youth Tunic (fits small teen): Two yards of fabric. Cut one piece twenty-four by forty-eight inches.

Adult Tunic (fits average-sized adult): Three yards of fabric. Cut one piece thirty-six by seventy-two inches.

Fold the fabric in half and mark the midpoint. Fold the fabric in half the other way and mark the midpoint. Lay the fabric flat on the floor, and place a small salad plate for the child and youth tunic and a large dinner plate for the adult tunic centered over the two markings. Trace the plate with a marker or pencil. Cut out the circle and discard. Trim edges as needed. Fit the tunic over the head of the child or adult. If the hole you have cut for the head is too small, cut a three-inch slit in the back as shown.

Head Scarf (Mary, Joseph, shepherds, and Wise Men)

Supplies needed: lightweight fabric, scarves, dish towel, rope, stretchy headbands

Cut a piece of fabric thirty-six by thirty-six inches. (Finish the edges as needed.) Head scarves can be worn in many different ways. See individual characters for head scarf options.

Sash #1 (Mary, angel)

Supplies needed: lightweight fabric, scarves, wide ribbon or rope

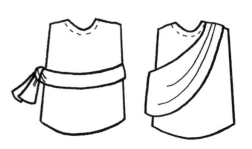

Cut a strip out of a contrasting fabric six by forty-eight inches (child), six by seventy-two inches (youth/adult). The sash will be tied around the tunic at the waist (wide ribbon, a scarf or rope may also be used). Finish the edges as directed above, if desired.

Sash #2 (Joseph, shepherd, Wise Man 1)

Cut a sash six by forty-eight inches (child), six by seventy-two inches (youth/adult). Glue or sew the ends together to make a loop of fabric. Finish the edges as desired. Wear the sash slung over one shoulder.

Wrap (Mary, Shepherd, Wise Man 2)

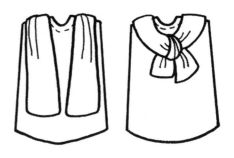

Cut a strip of fabric eight by thirty-six inches (child) twelve by sixty inches (youth/adult). Choose a more elegant fabric for the kings, jewels, fringe, or other embellishments.

Finish edges as desired (or intentionally fray the edges for a more rustic and worn look for the shepherds). Apply fringe or other decorative elements to the wrap for the Wise Men. The wrap is worn over the shoulders and is either tied in the front or allowed to drape.

Hair, Mustaches, Beards (Joseph, shepherds, and Wise Men)

Supplies needed: fake fur, scissors, ribbon or shoelace, rubber bands, double-sided sticky tape, grease pencil

Option 1: Purchase a beard. (Online options abound as well as discount stores, party and costume stores, and dollar stores.)

Option 2: Make a beard by cutting a scrap of fur fabric to the desired shape. Cut a half-inch slit one inch from the top corners of the beard. Tie a piece of yarn, ribbon, or a shoelace through the hole. Tie the beard on Joseph by draping the strings over the ears and tying at the nape of the neck. With the beard in place, estimate where the opening for the mouth would go, and cut a slit three inches wide by one inch high in the beard. Trim as needed.

Option 3: Loop a large rubber band through the hole as shown, and wrap the rubber band over the ears.

Option 4: Cut the fur to the desired shape. Attach to the face using double-sided tape. This works best for mustaches and goatees.

Option 5: Use face paint or a grease marker to draw on desired facial hair.

Animal Covers

Supplies needed: fabric (gray for the donkey, white for the sheep and camel, and other colors or patterns as desired)

Cut a large square of fabric forty-five by sixty inches. Finish the edges as desired. Cut another strip of the same fabric six by forty-eight inches (child), six by seventy-two inches (youth/adult) for a sash. The cover is worn by tying the corners of one end of the fabric over the shoulders and knotting them in front (like a cape). Tie the sash around the waist.

Animal Hats

Supplies needed: knit hats (white, gray, and brown), cotton balls, brown yarn, thick gray or black yarn, felt (white, gray, brown, and black), balloon, scissors, hot glue gun

Sheep Hat

Cut two ears using the pattern provided on page 69 out of white or black felt. Fold the ear in half and run a bead of hot glue along the bottom edge of the ear piece. Inflate a balloon, and put the hat on the balloon (this will make it easier to attach the ears and wool/fur). Place the balloon into a pot or bowl to steady it. Glue the ear two inches from the center of the top of the white knit hat so that the fold is facing the back of the hat. Repeat with the other ear. Place a large amount of glue all over the crown of the hat. Place cotton balls in the glue. Add more cotton balls and glue as desired.

Donkey Hat

Repeat the steps given for the sheep, using the gray hat. Cut two strips of gray or black felt three by twelve inches. Round the edges on one end of the piece of felt. Taper the other end by cutting as shown. Finish the ears by folding the ear in half (the long way, like a hot dog bun), and gluing the bottom edge, and attaching as directed in the instructions for the sheep hat. Cut several strips of thick gray or black yarn four inches long. Glue these strips to the crown of the hat to create a shock of hair on the top of the donkey's head.

Camel Hat

Cut two ears using the pattern provided out of brown felt. Follow instructions for gluing and assembling the ears on the sheep hat. Cut several strips of brown yarn and glue them all over the crown of the camel hat. Add more glue and strips of yarn as desired to make a thick shock of hair on top of the camel's head.

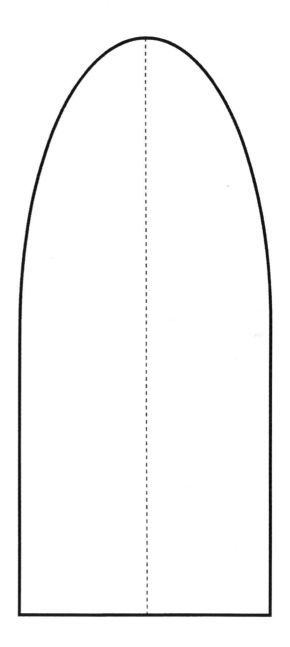

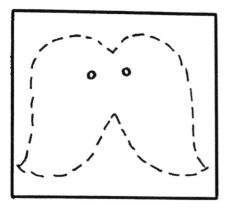 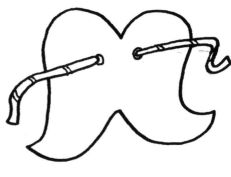

Angel Wings

Supplies needed: paper plates, two wire hangers, queen-sized white nylon stocking, white duct tape, white or gold ribbon, white or gold poster board

Option 1: Purchase commercially made angel wings online or at a party and costume supply shop.

Option 2: Make angel wings out of paper plates as shown on Day 8 (see page 39).

Option 3: Cut angel wings out of a large sheet of poster board. Laminate the wings, and punch two small holes approximately twelve inches apart in the middle of the wings. Thread three yards of ribbon up through one hole and back through the other. Adjust the ribbon so that the ends are even. With the wings on the back of the angel, bring the ribbon ends around to the front, and cross them over the opposite shoulder. Cross the ribbon ends again, and bring them around the front and tie at the waist.

Option 4: Straighten a wire hanger so that it has an oblong (balloon) shape and the hook is straightened as shown. Pull the white nylon stocking over the hangar frame, and adjust until the stocking is tight. Tape or glue the end as needed to secure it in place. Repeat with the other hanger. Place one wing on top of the other and tape the two ends together using the duct tape to secure the two wings together and cover all exposed wires. Wrap the duct-taped end of the wings with ribbon if desired. Adjust the wings by bending each away from one another. Tie a ribbon (three yards) around the bottom of the wings so that each end of the ribbon is of equal length. Tie the wings onto the angel as directed in option 3. Bring the ribbon over the shoulders, cross the ribbon in between the wings, and bring them over the base of the wings around to the front to tie.

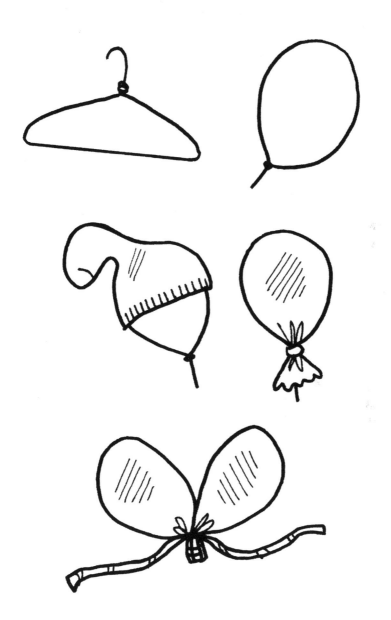

Putting It All Together

Mary

- *tunic*
- *sash*
- *head scarf*
- *wrap*

To wear the scarf, place the scarf on the head so that the edge is mid-forehead. Take the corners of the scarf behind the head, and tie into a knot under the draped scarf at the nape of the neck. A headband or rope may be tied around the head over the top of the scarf as shown.

Joseph

- *tunic*
- *sash:* use the looped sash and wear it by draping the sash over one shoulder.
- *head scarf:* place the scarf on the head so that the scarf frames the face.
- *headband:* a headband or rope may be tied around the head over the top of the scarf.
- *beard*

Shepherd

- *tunic*
- *sash or wrap*
- *headscarf:* To wear the scarf, place the scarf on the head so that the edge is mid-forehead. Put the headband around the head (make sure there is two inches of the scarf edge below the headband), and

roll and tuck the edge of the scarf over the headband to frame the face as shown.

- *headband*

- *beard:* wear a beard, goatee, or other facial hair as desired.

Angel

- *tunic*

- *sash*

- *wings*

- *halo:* To make a halo, create a loop out of gold tinsel. Glue the ends together and lay on top of the head or secure with clips or bobby pins.

Wise Men

- *tunic*

- *sash (either option)*

- *headscarf:* Headscarves may be worn as shown with Joseph or the shepherds. You can also use an extra sash and wrap it like a turban around the head. A crown may also be worn (purchase or make one), if desired.

- *headband*

- *beard:* Any style of beard or mustache may be worn.

Sheep

- *white sheep wrap and sash:* Tie it over the shoulders like a cape. Tie the sash around the waist.

- *sheep hat*

- *sheep tail:* Use the sheep ear pattern to make a tail. Cut the sheep tail out of white felt. Glue several cotton balls to the bottom edge. Attach the tail to the back of the sheep with a safety pin.

Donkey

- *gray wrap and sash:* Tie it over the shoulders like a cape. Tie the sash around the waist.

- *donkey hat*

- *donkey tail:* Cut eighteen strands of thick gray or black yarn twenty-four inches long. Knot all the strings together on one end. Working with six strands at a time, braid the yarn, and knot the end with six inches of string at the end. Attach the tail to the back of the donkey with a safety pin.

Camel

- *brown wrap and sash:* Tie it over the shoulders like a cape. Tie the sash around the waist.

- *balloons:* Inflate two balloons. Tie them together and pin to the shirt with a safety pin. Pull the wrap over the balloons and tie at the shoulders. The balloons will create humps for your camel.

- *camel hat*

- *camel tail:* See directions under "Donkey," using brown yarn instead of gray.

Neighborhood Celebrations

Have you ever wondered why you and your neighbors or friends spend so much time exchanging gifts with one another? I have often laughed at the amount of time and effort that I put into those gifts, carefully packaging a bunch of cookies, knowing that they're all doing the same for me. While appreciated (who doesn't love getting a pan of hot cinnamon rolls on a cold night?), I have wondered about the craziness of it. Why not gather together and do something different to celebrate Christmas with the Savior as friends and neighbors this year? Here are some ideas of things you can do to show your love for one another:

- Estimate what you would have spent on neighbor gifts, and then as a group, donate that amount to an agreed-upon charity.

- Challenge your friends and neighbors to perform an act of service as a family in the months leading up to the Christmas season. Pick an evening to gather together for hot chocolate and cookies to share that experience of service. You can have each family share with the group, or keep it anonymous by putting experiences on a card and placing the written experiences in a fishbowl upon arrival. After a potluck dinner or dessert, read the service experiences to the group.

- Have a neighborhood Christmas pageant. Choose one child to be Joseph and another to be Mary, and then invite others to dress up as any of the nativity characters they like. Adults can serve as townspeople, livestock, and so on. (See the "Nativity Dress-Up" section on page 64 for nativity costume ideas.) Those who don't wish to participate are encouraged to come and watch. This may mean you have several angels and a whole flock of sheep, but that just adds to the fun of the evening. Use the "Nativity Pageant" script (see page 62), or write your own. If you don't have a home large enough for all your neighbors to gather, have it outdoors on the lawn. Decorate with twinkle lights, and bring chairs and blankets to view the pageant. When the kids were little, we often had arguments about who got to be which character. To alleviate the contention, we began having the kids draw numbers from a bowl. Those numbers correspond with a similarly numbered bag that has all the dress-up components necessary for one of the Nativity characters. It's always fun to see who shows up as the angel. And of course, Dad often ends up as the donkey.

- Plan a neighborhood Nativity night, and have each family prepare one way to share the Nativity. This could be through a puppet show, song, video, and so on.

- Instead of exchanging cookies or bottles of hand soap, make a plan to offer to exchange simple acts of service, such as babysitting, carpooling, and so on. You can either perform that service for each friend, or draw names to choose one specific family in your group to serve. Remember that service doesn't have to be completed in December.

- Go on a Nativity walk. You can plan this to be an outdoor activity at a park if the weather is warm enough, or you can plan to travel from house to house in your neighborhood. Make arrangements with other friends or neighbors to celebrate the Nativity walk with you. Assign each house a different Nativity character to represent. If fewer than twelve families participate, you'll need to winnow down the list of Nativity characters to the most important few, or have each house double up on characters. Each child participating will need their own bucket or small gift bag for collecting items. Make a copy of the scripture card for each Nativity character. Place a picture on the door of the family who is sponsoring that Nativity character. All the children (and a few adults for supervision) gather at one home to begin. As the children stop at each door, they should greet the homeowner with a carol, and the homeowner, in turn, tells a short story, or engages the children in a short activity to represent each character. Suggested activities can come from the 12-Day Nativity activity ideas. Each home should also provide a small token to represent each character (a bag of wool for the sheep, a small star, and so on) for the children to collect. Inexpensive miniature nativity sets can be found at discount stores and would be a fun addition to the activity so that each child has his or her own nativity after visiting all the homes. At the last house, read or tell the Nativity story, or have the children retell the story by selecting one of the tokens from their bags and tell the narrative for that item. Finish off the night with a festive holiday treat together.

To create this adventure outside, designate different stations by attaching the scripture cards to a wooden or metal stake and placing the stakes around a park or open field. One adult mans each station with an activity and a token, and the children can travel together or in small groups from one station to the other. Decorate a pavilion or meeting area with twinkle lights for an extra festive finish.

Advents

Advent comes from the Latin word meaning "coming." It is a celebration of the waiting and expectation of the arrival of Jesus, both at His birth and also at His Second Coming. A new candle is lit each week for the four Sundays before Christmas as devotionals and scriptures are shared, learning of four virtues of Christ (hope, faith, joy, and peace). Occasionally accompanied by fasting, Advent is a time for reflecting on your relationship with God.

Four candles are added to an Advent wreath, one for each Sunday leading up to Christmas. Three are typically purple, with one being rose-colored. Sometimes, a white candle is set in the center of the wreath. While the scriptures and devotionals may differ from one faith to another, generally the candles are as follows:

- Week one: The prophecy candle is lit (purple). It is the candle of hope and the promise that Jesus is coming.

- Week two: The Bethlehem candle is lit (purple). It is the candle of faith and tells of the journey to Bethlehem.

- Week three: The shepherd candle is lit (rose). It is the candle of joy and tells of the joy at the birth of the Savior.

- Week four: The angel candle is lit (purple). It is the candle of peace and tells of the angels announcing the birth of the Savior.

- The white candle is lit on Christmas Eve and is the purity candle. It reminds us that Jesus is the Light of the World.

Advent is a time of waiting. As you find yourself in situations where you are waiting during this Christmas season (waiting in line, waiting for the Christmas concert to start, waiting for a package to arrive), use the time to reflect on your relationship with the Savior. Psalm 46:10 says, "Be still, and know that I am God." Do you feel hope, faith, joy, and peace? If not, reflect on one thing you can do today to restore one or more of those Christlike virtues into your life as you wait on His promised blessings.

You can create your own Advent wreath using a variety of materials. There are multiple examples of simple Advent wreath crafts online that you can do together as a family.

The Christmas Advent calendar is based on the celebration of Advent. Most begin on December 1 and continue every day throughout December. There are many different kinds available. Here are a couple that may help bring you closer to the Savior this Christmas.

Scripture Advent

Use the following scriptures about the Savior (or add a few of your own) as an advent to count down the days until Christmas. Some are prophetic verses about His birth and life; others are from His ministry. You could place each scripture on a piece of paper. Try burning the edges of the paper by briefly lighting them on fire to singe the edges to create a burned-edge effect. (Do this near a sink to avoid any out-of-control fire mishaps.) Roll each note up and tie with a string to a candle, and place all the candles in a large box or basket. Have family members take turns choosing a scripture, reading it, and then sharing their thoughts or feelings about what the scriptures say. Light the candle, and let it burn as you read. Add the candle to your collection each day so you will have a table full of lit candles by Christmas Eve.

1. Matthew 1:21	14. John 15:12
2. Acts 3:24, 26	15. John 14:27
3. Isaiah 9:6	16. John 16:33
4. Isaiah 7:14	17. Revelation 1:17–18
5. John 10:14	18. Isaiah 53:5
6. John 14:9	19. Mark 6:34
7. Luke 19:10	20. Job 19:25
8. Hebrews 1:1–3	21. Isaiah 40:11
9. Luke 2:40	22. Isaiah 12:2
10. Matthew 11:28–30	23. Luke 4:18
11. Matthew 25:31	24. 1 Corinthians 15:22
12. John 6:38	25. John 3:17
13. 1 John 4:14	

Symbols of Christmas Advent

Many of the symbols we see in our secular Christmas traditions also have sacred meanings. Collect a small trinket, ornament, or picture of the Christmas symbols—one for each day of the month of December leading up to Christmas Eve. Wrap each item individually and place them in a basket. Items can be hung on a small tree or on a piece of ribbon across a wall or doorway. Or you can make a Christmas tree box tower and place each item in the tower as you unwrap them. Take turns opening the objects, and share the sacred meaning as you add each one.

To make a Christmas tree box tower, you will need twenty-five small boxes that are approximately three by three inches (these can be found at dollar or discount stores). The boxes will be stacked on top of one another to create a tree shape as shown. On the bottom row, stack seven boxes side by side so that the boxes are on their sides and the opening of the box is facing forward. Glue the boxes together. For the second row, stack six boxes together as directed for the first row, and stack them on top of the first row. Center the second row of boxes over the first. You will need five boxes for the third row, four boxes for the fourth row, two boxes for the fifth row, and one box for the top. Glue all the boxes together, centering each row on top of the existing tower. Add a big ribbon around the tree box tower or add other embellishments as desired. If a uniform color is desired, paint the completed tower of boxes. Collect the following symbols[1] for your tree box tower (listed by symbol and description):

1. *Evergreen sprig.* Evergreen trees are green year-round, reminding us that God's love never ends. The needles on the evergreen point upward to heaven.

2. *Star.* The star reminds us of the Bethlehem star—a symbol to follow and search after the Savior.

3. *Candle.* The candle reminds us of the Light of Christ, which is a light to the world in darkness.

4. *Wreath.* The wreath is a reminder of the crown of thorns that was placed on the Savior's head before His crucifixion. Wreaths are also a colorful contrast to the cold and drab winter—a symbol of hope in uncertain times.

5. *Round ornament.* The round ball ornament is to remind us of God's creation—the earth and of His love that never ends.

6. *Holly leaves.* The sharp leaves of the holly tree remind us of the sharp thorns in the crown placed on Jesus's head at His Crucifixion. Holly was thought anciently to ward off evil, much like following the Savior does for us today.

7. *Presents.* Presents remind us of the gifts that the Wise Men brought the baby Jesus and also that the Savior is God's gift to the world.

8. *Candy cane.* The candy cane reminds us of the shepherd's crook, which helps the shepherd bring back sheep who are lost or who have gone astray; it is a symbol of how the Savior (the Good Shepherd) wants to draw us back when we become lost or stray from Him.

9. *Bells.* The bell is symbolic of the angels heralding the coming of the Savior at His birth.

10. *Red.* The Christmas color of red is to remind us of the blood of Christ, which was shed for us.

11. *White.* The Christmas color of white is to remind us of the purity of Christ.

12. *Green.* The Christmas color of green is to remind us of eternal life.

13. *Twinkle lights.* The lights on our trees and houses remind us of the Savior, lighting the way for us. It is a symbol of safety and peace.

14. *Stockings.* The stocking hung by the chimney is a reminder of those who do not have the necessary basics of life, like food and clothes. It is a reminder to us to reach out to those in need.

15. *Dove.* The dove is a symbol of peace. It reminds us that the Savior came to the world and will come again to bring peace.

16. *Mistletoe.* Mistletoe was once thought to bring protection to those who possessed it. Our faith in the Savior can bring us protection.

17. *Poinsettia.* The poinsettia's leaves turn red at Christmastime and are star-shaped. This is a symbol of the Bethlehem star, and its beauty is a symbol of God's beautiful creations. There is a legend that tells of how the poinsettia gets its red color that you may want to look up.

18. *Snowflake.* A snowflake's six-sided structure is a reminder that God created the earth in six days. It reminds us that each one of us is unique in God's eyes and that He can do great work with small things.

19. *Bow.* The bow is a symbol of God's love. We are bonded or tied to Him through His love for us.

20. *Hard candy.* Hard candy is a reminder that Jesus is our rock and that the gospel is sweet.

21. *Fruitcake.* Fruitcake reminds us of the twelve fruits of the Spirit—those characteristics that bring us closer to God (charity, joy, peace, patience, kindness, goodness, long-suffering, mildness, faith, modesty, purity, and chastity).

22. *Gingerbread man.* The gingerbread man reminds us that, like the gingerbread is created by man, mankind is created by God. The spices in gingerbread make it the color of the earth, which was also created by God.

23. *Wrapping paper.* Wrapping paper reminds us that God's gifts for us must be sought after and unwrapped. It also reminds us that what is on the inside is more valuable than the packaging that it comes in. We are more valuable to the Savior than our "wrapping" sometimes indicates.

24. *Christmas carols.* The Christmas carols remind us of the heavenly hosts that heralded the birth of the baby Jesus.

25. *Christmas cookies.* All the Christmas goodies (cookies, bread, rolls, and so on) remind us that the Savior is the bread of life and that the gospel is sweet.

Nativity Advent Calendar

One of the beloved Christmas decorations at my mother-in-law's home is the nativity Advent calendar. It is a felt banner that has numbered pockets. Each pocket holds a treasured piece of the nativity. Each night a new piece is extracted from a pocket and added to the nativity, with the littlest sheep often ending up perched on top of the stable. It has seen many years of love, and more than one of the siblings has their eye on it as their future inheritance. You can make a similar nativity Advent calendar to use in your home using the directions and pattern pieces provided. Instructions are given for gluing and sewing, depending on your personal preference.

Supplies needed: chalk, felt (one yard, neutral color, can be purchased where fabric is sold), felt squares—a variety of colors (these will be used to make individual nativity characters), twenty-four-inch dowel, decorative rope or ribbon, permanent markers, scissors, craft glue or hot glue, tape measure or ruler, sewing pins, sewing machine or thread and needle (optional), iron, iron-on numbers one through twenty-four (optional)

1. Cut a felt piece that is eighteen inches wide and twenty-six inches tall. You can choose to either sew your calendar or glue it together.

2. On one end (eighteen inches wide), turn the bottom edge under a half inch (one centimeter). Pin the edge in place and then press this edge flat with an iron. Glue or stitch this bottom edge.

3. Fold over the top edge one-and-a-half inches (four centimeters). Pin and press this edge flat with an iron. (Make sure that this edge is folded over on the same side as the bottom edge, leaving the front side with no edges or seams.) Glue or stitch along the edge one inch from the top, as shown.

4. Cut four strips of felt three by eighteen inches wide.

5. Using a piece of chalk and a ruler, mark vertical lines at three-inch intervals along the bottom fifteen inches of the advent calendar. (Make sure the edges that were turned under are on the underside when you do this.)

6. Using a piece of chalk and a ruler, mark horizontal lines at three, four, seven, eight, eleven, and twelve inches from the bottom of the calendar. This grid will be the markings to help you align the pockets.

7. Place one three by eighteen inches strip along the bottom edge of the advent calendar (the side with no edges or seams showing). Pin and stitch or glue along the bottom edge.

8. Fold the strip back, and lay a bead of glue (or stitch) along the three, six, nine, and twelve-inch lines along the bottom of the calendar—just up to the three-inch horizontal line, and press the strip flat on the advent calendar.

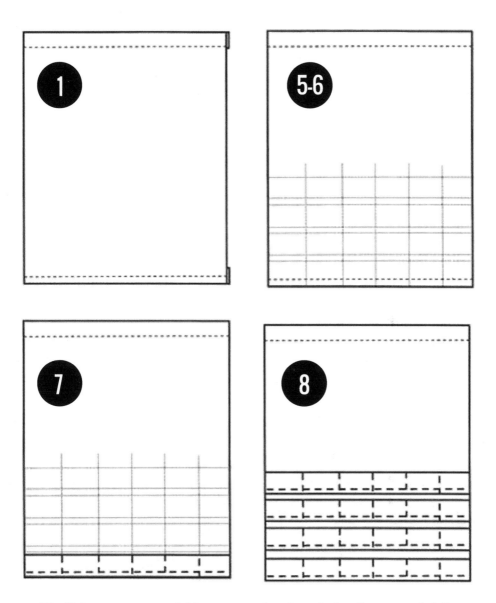

(You'll have to move quickly so your glue doesn't dry. See example.) Repeat this process, placing the next rows at the four, eight, and twelve-inch chalk lines.

9. Glue or stitch the outside edges. This should give you a bottom row of six pockets.

10. Repeat for the next three rows, leaving a one-inch gap between each row of pockets. Start row two at the four-inch line, row three at the seven-inch line, and row four at the eleven-inch line.

11. Glue or stitch along the outside edges of the advent to secure all the pockets.

12. Remove all exposed chalk lines with a damp cloth.

13. Once you have all the rows in place, you should have a total of twenty-four pockets. Using a permanent or fabric marker (or iron-on numbers), number each pocket one to twenty-four, starting with the first pocket on the top left as pocket 1.

14. Slide a twenty-four-inch dowel into the opening at the top of the Advent calendar. Tie a twenty-four-inch length of decorative rope or ribbon to each end and place a dot of glue under each to secure the ribbon to the dowel.

15. Cut four pieces of the stable pattern out of a brown- or tan-colored felt. Make wood grain markings on the stable if desired. Glue the stable to the front of the nativity Advent calendar, placing two pieces vertically about nine inches apart and about one inch above the top row of pockets. Lay the other two pieces on top of the sides of the stable to create a roof, as shown.

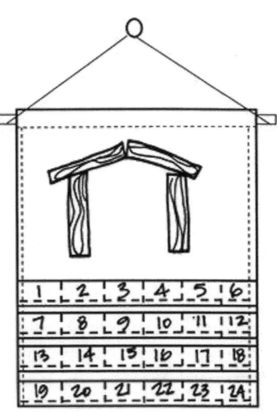

16. Use the rest of the pattern pieces to create the nativity figures. Use the scissors to cut the felt and hot glue to glue pieces together as needed. You may also want to add embellishments, such as jewels, glitter, yarn, or other items to add texture and dimension. You should have one of the following to put in each pocket:

1. Mary

2. Joseph

3. manger

4. hay

5. star

6. angel

7. Bethlehem city 1

8. Bethlehem city 2

9. shepherd

10. shepherd's crook

11. sheep 1

12. sheep 2

13. sheep 3

14. sheep 4

15. Wise Man 1

16. Wise Man 2

17. Wise Man 3

18. gold

19. frankincense

20. myrrh

21. camel

22. donkey

23. ox

24. baby Jesus

Place each character into a separate pocket (you may need to roll a few of the larger items up in order to fit it into the pockets). You can put them in any order desired; just make sure that the baby Jesus is in pocket twenty-four so He can be added to the nativity on Christmas Eve. Start your Christmas nativity Advent on December 1, and beginning on the second day of December, remove one item from a pocket each day until Christmas Eve.

Nativity Advent Calendar: Stable and Bethlehem Pattern

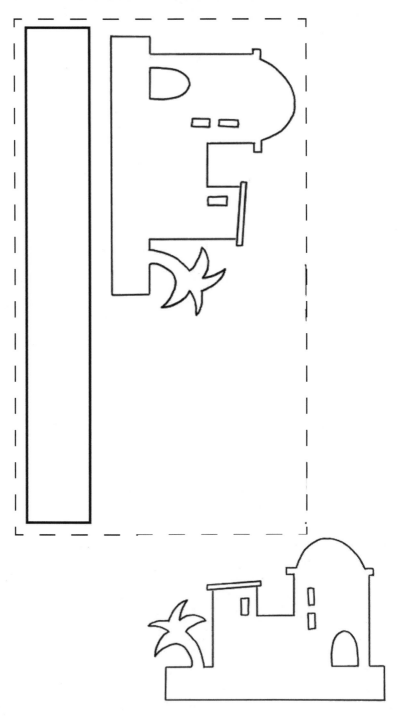

Nativity Advent Calendar: Donkey and Camel Pattern

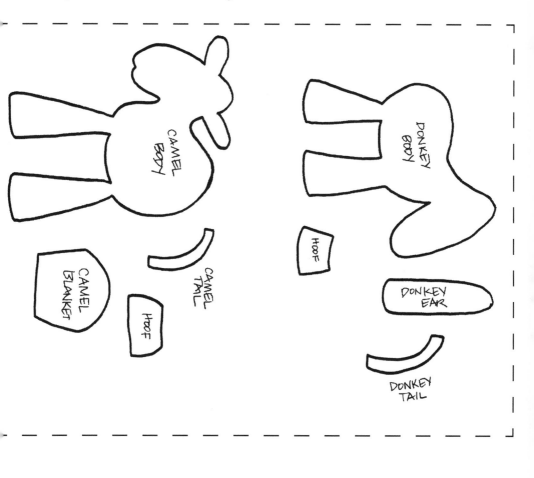

CAMEL BODY

DONKEY BODY

HOOF

CAMEL BLANKET

CAMEL TAIL

HOOF

DONKEY EAR

DONKEY TAIL

Nativity Advent Calendar: Sheep, Ox, and Star Pattern

Nativity Advent Calendar: Basic Body Pattern and Manger

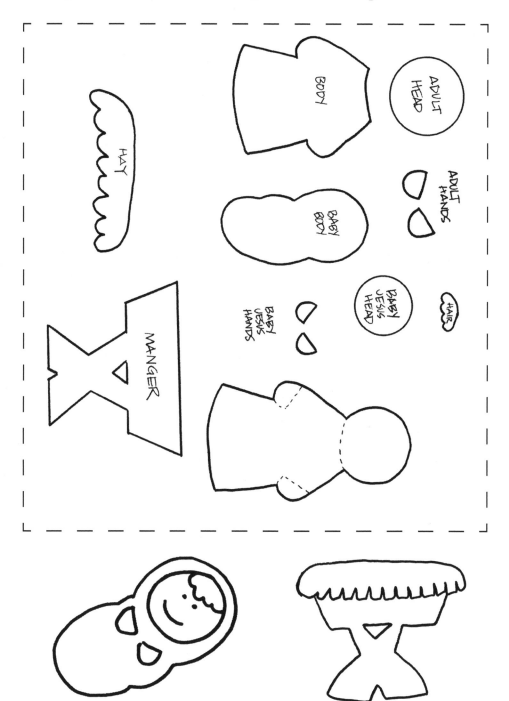

Nativity Advent Calendar: Accessories Pattern

Nativity Advent Calendar: Wise Men Accessories Pattern

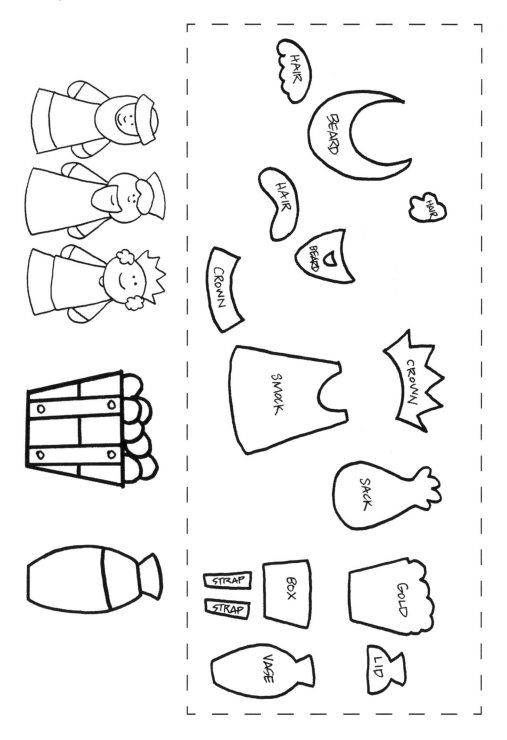

Other Ways to Celebrate the Nativity

Ornament Tree

Start collecting ornaments that depict the Nativity story. Let each child pick out a Nativity ornament each year, or make one out of crafting materials There are dozens of tutorials online. Ideas for ornaments could include scripture cards (see pages XX–XLIII) or key verses from the scriptural Nativity story in a decorative font. Add to a small frame and hang the frames from the branches in between the ornaments. Mix in with your regular ornaments, and after a few years, you'll have enough to decorate an entire tree in Nativity ornaments. Let each child pick out a new ornament each year to add to the collection.

Nativity Bracelet

Supplies needed: pipe cleaner, assortment of beads (one to represent each figure of the Nativity story—for example, a brown bead for the shepherd; yellow for the star; white for the angel; purple, red, and gold for the Wise Men; and so on)

Slide the beads onto the pipe cleaner in the order they appear in the Nativity story. Use the beads to help retell the story, moving each bead from one side of the bracelet to the other as you add each character to the story.

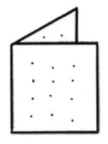 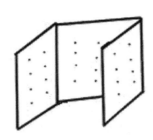 

Gingerbread Nativity

Supplies needed: graham crackers, sugar, shallow saucepan, stovetop, frosting, toothpicks, paper plates, assorted candies and snack items (see some of the following suggestions)

Instead of creating a gingerbread house, create a gingerbread nativity. To build the stable out of graham crackers, heat sugar over low heat until completely melted and amber in color. *Caution:* Working with melted sugar should be done only by adults. The sugar gets extremely hot and will burn you if it gets on your skin. Keep the heat low or the sugar will burn in the pan. Break one graham cracker in half. Dip one end of the halved graham cracker, and one short end of a regular graham cracker into the melted sugar. Quickly and carefully stand them up against one another on a paper plate to make the back and sides of the stable so that both ends that you dipped in the sugar are touching one another. Dip the other halved graham cracker in the sugar and attach it to the other side of the long graham cracker. Drip a spoonful of melted sugar down the seam where the two crackers meet if needed to secure the two sides together. For the roof, dip two regular-sized graham crackers at the short ends, and then hold the two sugared ends together to make an angled roof. Hold the crackers together for a minute until the sugar hardens. Drip a bead of sugar on the top of the side walls of the stable. Set the roof on top, and allow all the sugar to cool and harden.

Note: royal frosting can also be used to secure the graham crackers together, but it will take a few hours to set and harden, so plan accordingly if you plan to use the royal frosting rather than the sugar glue method. Alternatively, you can glue the pieces together with a hot glue gun, but recognize that this option is not edible, so if there's a chance little people will want to eat pieces of their ginger-bread house later, stick with one of the two food-safe options.

Finish off your gingerbread nativity by using candies and snack foods to create the characters of your gingerbread nativity. For example, you may want to cover the roof and sides of your stable with pretzel sticks, and use shredded wheat for the hay. Characters can be made out of large marshmallows, gum-drops, fruit roll ups, and so on to create bodies, hair, and robes. A miniature candy cane can be used for the shepherd's crook, a lifesaver for the angel halo, and a marshmallow rolled in frosting and white nerds for a cute sheep. Let your family get creative as they build their gingerbread nativity. Use buttercream frosting to attach all the candies to the stable.

Nativity for Little Fingers

Using the patterns for the nativity Advent (see pages 86–91), create felt fig-ures that little hands can manipulate. Cut a large rectangle of felt and add the stable as directed. Attach the felt rectangle to a wall or door down low at your child's eye level and have a small basket nearby with all the figures. (See "Nativity Advent Calendar" pages 82–91 for directions on making the figures.) Little ones will enjoy hours of moving, adding, removing, and rearranging the characters over and over again.

Variation: Print out a copy of all the nativity figures (pages 95–97) on T-shirt transfers. Color with permanent markers and trim around each figure. Press the transfers onto felt with a hot iron as per package instructions. Cut out each figure individually and use them to attach to the felt nativity banner.

App for That

There are several different apps that allow your child to build their own nativity. These apps are available for both Android and Apple products and would be a fun quiet-time activity for kids.

Using the Nativity Figure Printouts

Charms: Print out the figures from the nativity (see pages 95–97) on Shrinky Dinks plastic sheets (available online or at stores selling crafting materials). Color the figures if desired with permanent marker, cut the figures out, and punch a hole in the top of each figure. Bake in the oven as directed per package instructions, and string the figures onto a piece of yarn or cording to create a nativity bracelet. Use the figures to tell the story of the Nativity.

Nativity puppets: Print out or copy the nativity figures, color as desired, laminate, and attach each figure to a craft stick to make stick figure puppets. Throw a blanket or table cloth over a table or box, and use the figures to create a nativity puppet show.

Nativity set: Print out or copy the nativity figures, and color as desired. Attach the figures to small painted wood blocks using Mod Podge (or attach the pictures to empty toilet paper rolls) to have your own stand-up nativity that little hands can manipulate.

Story: Use the nativity figures to make your own nativity book or as the illustrations for Christmas cards or gift tags.

Nativity story glove: On heavy cardstock, reduce the size of the nativity figures (see pages 95–97) so each figure is about one inch tall. Color as desired, and laminate for durability. Glue the bumpy or "sticky" side of a small piece of Velcro to the backs of each figure, and glue or sew the fuzzy side of a small piece of Velcro to each fingertip of a set of gloves. Lay the figures facedown on a tabletop in the order they appear in the Nativity story (Joseph, Mary, donkey, shepherd, sheep, angel, star, Wise Men). Put the gloves on your hands, and starting with your pinky finger on your right hand, press your finger down on the nativity figures as you tell the story. This way you can pick up all the figures without taking the gloves off, and the story will show on your fingers from right to left as the child faces you.

Nativity of love: Place a stack of assorted nativity figures in a bowl on the table along with markers or other writing implements. Encourage your family to write notes of love and encouragement to one another on the nativity figures.

Have your kids draw a stable on a piece of paper. Add the nativity figures to their scene, each creating their own nativity display with these notes of love. Read all the notes on the last day that you celebrate the 12-Day Nativity.

Nativity Treasure Hunt

While doing errands such as shopping or going to the library, give your children (and yourself) the assignment to keep an eye out for Nativity-related decorations, such as wrapping paper, signs, yard art or even holiday music that represents the Nativity. Decide on a point or token system for each item spotted to see who can find the most nativities or decorations every day.

Christmas Cards

As you select a Christmas greeting card this year, consider choosing one that depicts the Nativity and expresses your love of the Savior. You might have the children dress up as nativity characters for a photo card. Be sure to save one and frame it to hang on your nativity tree as a treasured memory from each year. (See "Symbols of Christmas Advent," page 79, and "Nativity Dress-Up," page 64.)

Keep a scrapbook of all the nativity cards you receive, or decoupage the images from the fronts of the cards onto the outside of your 12-Day Nativity box or ornament storage box. Mount individual photos onto thin pieces of wood or frame with craft materials to add as an ornament to your nativity tree. (See "Symbols of Christmas Advent," page 79.)

Swap Out the Elf

One Christmas activity is based on a popular book about a little elf dressed in red. The little elf hides and leaves a little mischievous fun behind. There are many posts on Pinterest and blogs detailing elaborate set up and schemes for the little elf. If you're going to spend all that time, money, and energy, consider using nativity characters instead. Using a separate nativity set that has been put out at the beginning of the month and play "Who is missing today?" Remove one character each day—the wandering Wise Men, the lost sheep, the shy shepherd—and hide them elsewhere in the house for the kids to find. Once the wayward character is found, it is returned to the nativity display, and a second character is chosen the next day. The kids will have to figure out who is missing and then search for that character. You can use similar scenes like those suggested for the elf or create nativity-themed hiding spots (hide the sheep under a pile of hay or fly the angel by a string from the ceiling fan, for example).

Share the Faith

Use this holiday season to share your faith, and allow your friends to share their faith traditions with you. Attend a church service or holiday program of another faith, and bring a friend. Or use this time to reconnect with your faith if you have grown distant. If you haven't prayed lately, use the daily devotionals as a nudge to offer a prayer of thanks through this holiday season.

Jesse Tree

The Jesse Tree is a celebration of the genealogy of Christ. (The first verses of Matthew 1 and Luke 1 list the lineage of Christ.) The Jesse Tree follows the chronology of the Bible and the anticipation of the coming of Christ. Each day, a Bible verse representing one of the Bible stories, starting with Adam, traces the genealogy down to the Savior. There are as many ways to celebrate as there are unique family traditions, but each story is a reminder of how God prepared the world for His coming. There are many online resources for downloadable ornaments and a list of Bible verses and thought-provoking questions to go with each day.

As a family, go out and find a branch and place it in a large bucket or container. Secure in place with some plaster of Paris. Using an online source or your own creations, make your own ornaments.

Use this as an opportunity to discover and explore your own roots. Where did you come from? What sacrifices have your ancestors made so that you could live the life that you do now? What decisions did you make in the past that have led you to where you are now? Can you identify a time when your faith in Christ was confirmed?

Share the Jesse Tree with your family this season, and find a way to share your family tree with your family.

Celebrating the Nativity around the World

There are many different traditions for celebrating the Nativity around the world.[2] While this is certainly not an exhaustive list, and the traditions and activities are often celebrated in small regions (not the entire country), here are a few fun traditions from around the world that you may want to try where you live. You may want to have a special nativity set that includes the elements of all of these different traditions.

Puerto Rico

Many Latin cultures like Puerto Rico celebrate *Misa del Gallo*, or "Mass of the Rooster," at midnight on Christmas Eve. It is called this because it is said that a rooster crowed to announce the birth of Jesus. After the midnight mass, churchgoers walk through the streets, carrying torches, playing instruments, and singing.

Celebrate the Nativity by gathering an assortment of musical instruments (or make some of your own, using objects like pots and pans for drums). Make torches by taping flashlights to the end of a long pole or dowel. Wrap the top of the flashlight with yellow cellophane so that it extends five to six inches above the flashlight. Give everyone a torch and a musical instrument and have a parade around your neighborhood at night, singing songs and crowing like roosters.

You may also want to make or find a rooster to hover over your Christmas celebration. Place it on a ledge or shelf near your Christmas nativity scene as a reminder of the announcement of the birth of the baby Jesus. If you are adding tokens of your worldwide traditions to your nativity set, find a small plastic rooster (or have one of your children draw a picture of a rooster and reduce it an appropriate size), and place it on the roof of your stable.

Poland

In Poland, spiders and spider webs are often used to decorate Christmas trees. This is because of a legend that tells of a spider that spun a blanket for the baby Jesus.

In addition to commercially made looms for kids, there are many different kinds of weaving looms that you can build out of straws, cardboard, paper plates, fingers, and so on. Instructions for using these looms can be easily found online. Choose one that suits your interest and weave a small blanket for the baby Jesus.

Weaving is difficult for small hands and will require a lot of hands-on help. Keep your project simple, or cut a small piece of fabric to cover the baby instead of weaving.

If you are adding tokens of your worldwide traditions to your nativity set, find a small plastic spider (or have one of your children draw a picture of a spider and reduce it an appropriate size) and place it in the stable and your blanket on the baby Jesus.

Russia

Russian legend tells of a *babushka* (a word for "grandmother") who decided not to travel with the Wise Men to see the baby Jesus. She regretted staying behind, and it is said that she is still searching for the baby Jesus and leaves presents for good children on her way.

Wrap a small gift in a box using a colorful scarf (or an eighteen-by-eighteen-inch square of colorful fabric) instead of traditional wrapping paper, and hide them in a nearby park (or in a room of the house if the weather is too cold). Take another scarf (or fabric) and cut it into one-inch strips. Starting from your doorstep (or a starting point in your home), tie a piece of fabric to a tree or shrub and then another to the next tree or shrub, a mailbox, or another fixed object. Leave several of these fabric scrap clues along the way to your final destination in your treasure hunt. Hide the scarf-wrapped gifts at your final destination. Tell the children the story of the *babushka*, and then, using the scarf clues, hunt down the gifts left by the *babushka*. Wear your scarves home.

If you are adding tokens of your worldwide traditions to your nativity set, find a colorful scarf or piece of patterned fabric and place it under your stable.

Germany

In some parts of Germany, children leave letters they have written to the Christ Child in their windowsills. Using one of the scripture cards (see page XX–XLIII) or the thank-you note (see page 57) or a piece of stationery, and have your children write notes to the Christ Child. Young children can draw pictures and dictate the words while you write them down on the paper for them. Place these notes in an envelope, and place them in the windowsill.

If you are adding tokens of your worldwide traditions to your nativity set, make a small envelope from a folded scrap of paper and add it to your stable.

Israel (Bethlehem)

As the town where Jesus was born, Bethlehem is a busy and festive place at Christmas. The Church of the Nativity is adorned with flags and decorations.

The Christmas Eve service features a dramatic procession of galloping horsemen—police on Arabian horses followed by a solitary horseman on a coal-black horse, carrying a cross. This parade travels through the city to the church. After entering the church, an ancient effigy of the Christ child is placed in the church. This event is so popular that people sit on rooftops and crowd in any space available to watch. After the services, churchgoers can follow the winding stairs that lead to a grotto that has a silver star to mark the place where Jesus was born.

A cross is painted over the door of Christian homes in Bethlehem, and each home displays a homemade nativity.

Cut a star or cross shape out of heavy cardstock paper. Paint the paper with glue and attach glitter. Hang the cross over your front door, and place the silver star underneath the baby Jesus in your nativity.

Costa Rica

The *portal* is a nativity scene made from natural materials such as twigs, grass, cork, mosses, and other materials such as glitter, colored papers, and colored sawdust. Small figurines of Mary, Joseph, the baby Jesus in the manger, and all the other typical characters are added, as well as farm animals, dolls, fruit, and other common items. The characters are all moved closer into the manger as the days draw closer to Christmas. The baby Jesus is added at midnight on Christmas Eve.

Create your own *portal* by covering a small shoe box with moss, twigs, grass, and other natural elements. Draw pictures of the characters (or copy and color those on pages 95–97) and add them to your *portal*. Make small fruits, dolls, or other common household items out of clay or play dough, and add them to you your *portal*.

Mexico

For nine days before Christmas, neighbors gather and travel from house to house each day in a *Posada* to act out Mary and Joseph's pilgrimage to Bethlehem. Travelers sing, pray, and share seasonal treats and tamales.

Purchase some fresh tamales (if they are available where you live), or try your hand at making them as you celebrate a *Posada* with your neighbors. (See "Neighborhood Celebrations" on page 75 for more neighborhood fun and celebrations.)

The legend of the poinsettia also comes from Mexico. Find a short version of this legend and share it with your family as you add a small poinsettia to your home, or make a pathway that leads to your nativity with poinsettia leaves.

Philippines

Parols are paper lanterns that are made in the shape of a star. The art of *parol* making is handed down from one generation to the next, and the *parols* are often placed outside of houses and carried through the streets during the Christmas season. The frame is made from bamboo and is covered with colored paper. Pom poms, tassels, and other decorations are added to the points of the star. They are often brightly lit.

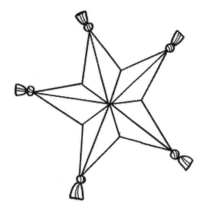

Make your own *parol* by creating a star shape with small twigs or bamboo. Cut up several strips of colored crepe paper. Glue the crepe paper to the star. Once it is dry, add yarn tassels to the tips of the star. Tie each *parol* with a loop and hang your colorful stars in a window with a string of twinkle lights to light them up.

If you are adding tokens of your worldwide traditions to your nativity set, make a small *parol* for your nativity set (you can use toothpicks instead of twigs), and hang it from the roof of your stable.

Ethiopia

Christmas is celebrated on January 7 in Ethiopia. As people arrive dressed in white for the Christmas Mass, they light a candle and circle the interior of the church three times.

Choose a night to celebrate Christmas in Ethiopia. Have everyone dress in white, and as they enter the designated room, have them hold a candle or flashlight as they circle the room. Sing your favorite Christmas hymns or carols, and find a recipe for an Ethiopian Christmas treat online to share.

If you are adding tokens of your worldwide traditions to your nativity set, find a small birthday candle and place it in your stable.

India

To prepare for Christmas, families clean their homes and churches and make any necessary repairs so everything is ready for the birthday of Jesus.

To prepare your home for the new baby, pick one room or area in your home that needs cleaning or repair. Work together as a family to clean and organize at least one space in your home. Make sure that everyone has a specific job. You may want to consider using this time to sort through clothes, books, and toys that no longer fit or are no longer used and find a charitable place to donate them. An alternative activity would be to clean up an elderly neighbor's yard, or pick up trash around your neighborhood to make it a more appealing place.

If you are adding tokens of your worldwide traditions to your nativity set, place a small sliver of soap in your stable.

Italy

In some regions of Italy, bagpipers dress up in costumes reflecting biblical times. They travel through the towns playing hymns and folk songs. These *zampognari* are often included in nativity scenes.

In some homes in Italy, the *presepe* ("nativity") holds a special place and is prominently displayed in the home. Children write a letter to their parents with promises to be good in the new year. These letters are read during the Christmas Eve feast and are sometimes burned so that good wishes and prayers will be sent up to heaven in the ashes.

Encourage your children to write a letter detailing how they hope to be a little better in the upcoming year. Use a fire pit or fireplace and light the fire. Add your letters to the fire if desired. (You may want to keep a copy of the letter from year to year as a keepsake.)

If you are adding tokens of your worldwide traditions to your nativity set, find a small toy bagpiper (or have one of your children draw or print a picture of a bagpiper online and reduce it an appropriate size) and place it in your stable.

Vietnam

In Catholic parishes in Ho Chi Minh City, people erect life-sized crib (nativity) scenes and decorate the whole street.

Encourage or challenge your neighbors to create festive decorations in their yards, and consider adding a life-size nativity to your collection for the front yard. See "Neighborhood Celebrations" (page 75) for other fun neighborhood celebrations.

Belgium

Advent (see pages 77–91) is popular among those who celebrate the Christmas Nativity. Many families also have paper Advents on the back of the front door to their home. These have little doors that hide small pieces of Belgian chocolate for each day of Advent leading up to Christmas.

Create your own doorway Advent using small pieces of Belgian chocolate for treats inside each day's door. You will need poster paper or heavy wrapping paper,

double-sided tape or white craft glue, chocolate, and a utility knife or scissors, and large stickers. Decide how big you want your Advent to be (whether it will cover the entire door or just a portion of it). Cut two equal lengths of poster paper. Cut a small template for the individuals door flaps out of cardboard (a three-by-three-inch square is suggested, but you can make yours a different size if you wish). Draw twenty-four doors on one of the papers using the cardboard pattern as a template. You can choose to place the doors in random spots or line them up in rows. Number each door one through twenty-four. Let your children decorate the rest of this sheet of poster paper as desired. Using the utility knife or scissors, cut around both sides and the top of each door. Turn this paper face-down on a table or on the floor. Using the double-sided tape or a thin line of craft glue, outline the edges of each of the doors. With a partner, lay the second piece of poster paper over the first, lining up the edges and pressing down so that all the tape or glue sticks to the other paper. Once this is dry, turn the door advent over and pull each flap open and place a small piece of chocolate inside. Secure each door shut with a large sticker or piece of tape.

If you are adding tokens of your worldwide traditions to your nativity set, leave a small piece of chocolate for the baby in your stable.

Nativity Books

One of the popular traditions for young families is to unwrap a Christmas-themed book each day as a countdown to Christmas. To keep your celebrations Christ-focused, consider investing (you can add a couple of titles each year) in Nativity-themed story books. You may want to coordinate that specific books be opened on particular days. For example, unwrap the *Father and Son* storybook on the day that you unwrap the Joseph figurine for your nativity.

This is by no means an exhaustive list, but it is a place to start. If you have young children, you will want to choose more simple board books. Older children will appreciate stories with a little more complexity.

Nativity books are a great way for grandparents to participate in the 12-Day Nativity. If you are a grandparent and want to share in your grandchildren's 12-Day Nativity experience from afar, order a Nativity book to be shipped for each day of the Nativity Advent, and have them delivered one day at a time for some excitement each day.

Here are a few titles that you might consider:

Father and Son: A Nativity Story, by Geraldine McCaughrean (Disney-Hyperion Books). This is the Nativity story told from Joseph's perspective of what he could offer his son, knowing that Jesus was the Son of God.

Star Bright: A Christmas Story, by Alison McGhee, (Athenum Books for Young Readers). A little angel wonders what to give the baby.

Song of the Camels, by Elizabeth Coatsworth and Anna Vojtech (NorthSouth). Beautifully illustrated, this book tells the tale of the camels that brought the kings to the baby Jesus. Best for older children.

Saint Francis and the Christmas Donkey, by Robert Byrd (Dutton Juvenile). Tells the legend of the donkey and how he was involved in the birth of the babe in Bethlehem. Best for older children.

How Many Miles to Bethlehem? by Kevin Crossley-Holland (Arthur A. Levine Books). Beautifully illustrated, this book details the story of the holy family fleeing from Herod.

The Donkey's Christmas Song, by Nancy Tafuri (Scholastic Press). The animals all sing, but the donkey brays and makes the baby laugh.

We Were There: A Nativity Story, by Eve Bunting (Houton Mifflin Harcourt). The Christmas story told by nontraditional animals who might also have been in the stable, such as a scorpion and a spider.

The Most Precious Gift, by Marty Crisp (Philomel). Beautifully illustrated, this book tells the tale of the Nativity from the perspective of a drummer boy.

The Christmas Star, by Marcus Pfister (NorthSouth). The tale of the star and how it brought the shepherds, Wise Men, and animals together to see the baby.

Humphrey's First Christmas, by Carol Heyer (Ideals Children's Books). Beautifully illustrated, this is the story of a camel and how he gives up his prized possession to the baby Jesus.

A Child Was Born: A First Nativity Book, by Grace Maccarone (Scholastic). The story of the Nativity told in rhyme.

Who is Coming to Our House? by Joseph Slate (Scholastic). Each animal does his or her part to prepare for the arrival of a mysterious guest.

The First Noel: A Christmas Carousel, by Jan Pienkowski (Candlewick). The story of the Nativity with pop-up paper illustrations. The book folds out into a carousel to tell the Christmas story.

The First Christmas, by Jan Pienkowski (Knopf Books for Young Readers). The Nativity story illustrated with dark silhouettes against beautifully colored backgrounds.

Child of the Promise, by Stormie Omartian (Harvest House Publishers). Illustrated for older readers, this book tells the full story, beginning with Isaiah.

The Last Straw, by Fredrick H. Thury (Charlesbridge). A proud old camel caries many gifts to the newborn King.

The Nativity, illustrated by Julie Vivas (HMH Books for Young Readers). Delightful and nontraditional illustrations of the Nativity story (the angel Gabriel with his tattered wings sits down with Mary in her house slippers to bring her the news).

The Birds of Bethlehem, by Tomie dePaola (Nancy Paulsen Books). The Nativity as told by a flock of colorful birds.

A Northern Nativity, by William Kurelek (Tundra Books). A young boy imagines the Nativity story happening in different times and different places, and he wonders who would have seen the miracle and bought the gifts and where the baby would lie.

Song of the Stars: A Christmas Story, by Sally Lloyd-Jones (Zonderkidz). All God's creations—plants, animals, and stars—anticipate and celebrate in song the coming of the newborn King.

Christmas in the Manger, by Nola Buck (HarperFestival). A board book that tells a simple version of the Nativity.

Room for a Little One: A Christmas Tale, by Martin Waddell (Margaret K. McElderry Books). There's always room for one more in the stable, and a kind ox makes room for one more weary traveler.

My Son, My Savior: The Awesome Wonder of Jesus' Birth, by Calvin Miller (Chariot Victor Publishing). The Nativity story told from Mary's perspective. Written for older readers.

The Animals' Christmas Eve, by Gale Wiersum (Golden Books). The animals in the barn all gather around to remember the story of the first Christmas.

One Baby Jesus: A New Twelve Days of Christmas, by Patricia A. Pingry (Candy Cane Press). The Nativity story told in the familiar Twelve Days of Christmas style. Board book for young children.

The Crippled Lamb, by Max Lucado (Tommy Nelson). God has a special place in the Nativity story for a little crippled lamb.

Notes

1. "Christmas Holidays" accessed July 23, 2015, www.celebratingholidays. com; Confraternity of Penitents, "The Christian Meaning of Christmas Symbols," accessed July 23, 2015, http://www.penitents.org/meaningchristmassymbols.html.

2. Natalie PlanetSmartyPants, "Christmas in Different Lands," last modified December 1, 2013, http://multiculturalkidblogs.com/2013/12/01/ christmas-in-different-lands/; "Christmas around the World," accessed July 27, 2015, www.Whychristmas.com; "Christmas Celebrations around the World," accessed July 27, 2015, http://www.teachingmom.com/features/christmasworld.html.

Journal

_____

_____

_____

_____

_____

_____

_____

_____

_____

_____

_____

_____

_____

_____

_____

_____

_____

_____

_____

_____

_____

_____

_____

_____

_____

_____

_____

_____

_____

_____

_____

_____

About the Author

Marilee Woodfield is an author, blogger, seminary teacher, early childhood educator, and one of the organizers of the Carrollton Community Nativity (TheCommunityNativity.com)—an interfaith display of over eight hundred *crèches* from around the world that attracts thousands of visitors annually. Her personal collection includes forty-one *crèches* from various countries. Her blog, *Frosted Insanity* (frostedinsanity.com), features fantastical cake creations she builds as a "hobby that pays for itself." She and her family live in Carrollton, Texas.